TRANSILIENCE

Powering Through Adversity To Find Happiness

Seven Qualities of Resilient Clients and Six Tools for Transilient Living

Kathryn Den Houter Ph.D.

Transilience: Powering Through Adversity
Copyright © 2017 Kathryn Den Houter, Ph.D.
ISBN: 978-0-9971530-9-5
Library of Congress: 2016920794

The inspiration for the transilient individuals came from my clients. However to secure their confidentiality and well-being, these accounts have been fictionalized, so they cannot be identified. I am deeply grateful for the willingness to share their lives and for the trust they have in me.

La Maison Publishing, Inc.
Vero Beach, Florida
The Hibiscus City
www.lamaisonpublishing.com

Endorsement for *Transilience: Powering Through Adversity*
By Kathryn Den Houter, Ph. D.

With experience and integrity, Kathryn Den Houter portrays the reality that faith plays in the journey of living a resilient life. Lifting up seven qualities, the reader is given examples of those who have navigated life's challenges as *transilient* people. This creative and thoughtful book is rounded out with study questions and exercises that teach the art of *transilience*. It is a hope-filled read, full of insight and wisdom for all who want to live in a thriving and abundant way.

Dr. Anne C. Hébert,
Pastor of St. Andrews Presbyterian Church, Beulah, MI

Transilience by Dr. Kathryn Den Houter provides a step-by-step path toward greater resiliency for everyone. An easy read, the book first discusses seven resilient-boosting traits with exercises to strengthen them. In the second part, she spells out simple methods for handling common life problems like stress and insomnia. Faith based groups, life coaches, and group counselors would find this a valuable resource and addition to their libraries.

Helen Smith Barnet, PhD,
Connecticut Psychologist and author of, Divorcing Again?

Preface

For over twenty-five years, I have worked as a clinical psychologist helping one person after another. When I first started my career, I was often puzzled why one individual would surmount unbelievable challenges and move on to lead a happy life, while the next seemed stuck with half the worries unable to muster the grit or sustain the therapeutic gains. What was it about some that gave them the edge at meeting life's challenges? Over time, seven clues surfaced, and I will call these resilient traits. When these resilient traits were combined with a transcendent spirituality, the transilient individual emerged. This combination was unstoppable.

Transcendence is the ability to see the big picture—to take an overview of your situation and see troubles as part of life that can be overcome with determination and insight. This transcendent view adds another dimension to life's struggles. Hence, the title of this book is *Transilience*.

Spirituality that transcends, is knowing

❖ that there is a relief in seeing the "big picture." It is understanding that something larger than the self is in control. Daily struggles are almost insignificant when a panoramic worldview is employed.

❖ that our problems are either solvable or manageable and that they are only temporary. They will not last forever because God offers us a glorious future.

❖ that the promises of God reign supreme, and that we believe that God can find ways to redeem the most horrible of circumstances. Heaven is the ultimate victory.

❖ that being a part of a community of faith, where burdens are shared in an honest fashion, lightens the load. We breathe easier.

❖ that those who regularly worship God, are happier people. [1]

❖ that prayer eases daily aches and worries and promotes better mental and physical health. [2]

❖ that meaningful relationships give us insights and add purpose to our lives. In the midst of the dark trials, we know God's sustaining presence will get us through. On the other side of this trial, there is a renewed purpose. This purpose might be listening to others with greater wisdom or giving to others who have been through similar struggles.

"Broken" people start therapy because they are looking for healing. An infinite variety of life events can trigger a need for therapy. It might be a loss of someone close, a job loss, a marriage breakup, an addiction problem, or a rebellious child in harm's way. What we know from our training as psychologists is that pain is a necessary precondition for change. It is not the easy, complacent life that forces us to change, but it is the painful parts of life. The seekers among us are often driven by this pain to find help. They are the ones who find the strength to change which results in a more productive life.

I'm not prone to put bumper stickers on my car, but when I started my private practice, I had some made that read: LOSERS COMPLAIN, WINNERS GET COUNSELING. Although simplistic, it reflected my

---

[1]

[2]

sentiment at the time. Victims stay victims because they don't reach out to make the necessary changes. Richard Rohr in his book, *Falling Upward* reveals that those of faith, direct their focus upward, toward God, rather than spiraling downward. Change is a necessary part of the spiritual life. "… if there isn't serious warning about the blinding nature of fear and fanaticism, your religion will always end up worshiping the status quo and protecting your present ego position and personal advantage—as if it were God! Jesus preached his first message, which is clearly, *Repent! Change!*" [3]

When hit by painful circumstances we become invested in our need to change. Our growth moves upward and forward until we hit another wall that requires another change. Our energy is reserved for our forward momentum rather than becoming bogged down by fear or blaming others. As we practice spiritual growing, "hitting the wall" becomes less traumatic and more like a constructive reflection gained through the obstacles of life. It becomes more like a smooth glide as we problem-solve through adversity. As we gain insights into our struggles and learn to power through them, we become "transilient."

Spirituality comes in many different forms. I am partial to the Christian faith, but arguably, other religious choices provide similar sustainability of treatment. Those faith-walks can best be described by those more intimately involved with those spiritual practices. I will be focusing on the Christian faith as I review the qualities of transilience.

3

Acknowledgements

I am so grateful to my clients who have been courageous seekers of the truth. Their invincible spirits have taught me so much. Without their honesty and valor, this book would not have been possible. The names have been changed to insure confidentiality.

In so many ways, my past twenty-five years of private practice have been blessed years. Every day I learned something new. Life was full of surprises. There were tears of both joy and sadness as my clients and I navigated through unchartered waters. Hallelujahs happened. Epiphanies and insights became even more significant when the end result was a closer walk with God.

The lives of my clients and their heroic efforts to overcome obstacles have inspired me to write this book. I thank you from the bottom of my heart.

Introduction

This is just the right time for such a book. We have a culture that demands adaptability, personal insights, and a willingness to change. Resilience is essential for optimum survival. From that experience, I reviewed my twenty-five years as a psychologist and identified seven resilient qualities. In this book, I chose eight of my most successful clients to represent these qualities. First and foremost, the overarching attribute among them was their faith. Either they came from families with a deep faith or they embraced it later in life. In any case, their resiliency was transilient.

The first of the seven qualities presented in this book is an ability to connect with nature. When times are tough and chaotic, the clients that survived found solace by walking in the woods, listening to the birds, contemplating the stars, and breathing in the fresh air. They used nature to rally, to think, to renew, and to energize. Sometimes, an hour with nature could be just as healing as an hour with a therapist. Nature's healing worked particularly well for children with attention problems. For adults, nature offered a new perspective: tranquility.

The second quality is the attitude of adventure. Inside these seekers you would hear "What's new? What's around the corner?" This creates an excitement-rich life. These thoughts click on the "beta," which is the brain wave that says you're onto something. This positive attitude is motivating and, most importantly, when it's activated, fear is almost nonexistent. Life becomes a thrill, filled with endless treasures. One's attitude is the key for overcoming adversity. Accepting the present, believing in the future, and repelling fear are components for this transilient quality. My clients with this attitude were too "blessed to be stressed," to use a homey phrase. They saw adversity as something to process through and not the endgame.

The third quality is what I call "dark walking." Transilient people learn how to walk through the dark. They learn to transform their nights of terror by gaining the strength they need to confront their fears. How we handle the dark is equivalent to how we handle losses. We become stronger when we treat "endarkenment" and enlightenment as parts of the whole, both as a portion of life.

The fourth characteristic is facing scarcity with creativity. Unfortunately, scarcity is a part of our lives. Whether it is needing more money, having a lack of friends, wanting better health, having too little education, or suffering an empty marital relationship, we find ourselves in short supply. How we deal with these insufficiencies is an indicator of our resiliency. Are we creative problem solvers or do we suffer passively?

The fifth transilient quality is the ability to connect with others, which is a strong predictor of an extraordinary life. This quality is particularly true for young children. Linda Goldman in her book *Raising Our Children to Be Resilient,* states: "A major aspect of resilience may be the feeling that 'I'm not totally alone against the world—that somehow, somewhere, I'm part of something bigger than me.' Regardless of which lens it is viewed through—spiritual, social, community, or family—resilience provides and encourages altruistic urges to help others and to make life work."[1] This is what I call "the relief of the big picture," finding comfort and knowing that you are not alone, but that you are a part of the whole context of life. You fit in the scheme of things. Around you are supportive people and, with this attitude, you are able to find them.

The sixth transilient quality discussed is the significance of reflection. Anyone who has faced struggles knows how hard it is to reflect on that past. It brings up shame, self-questioning, and uncertainty, but this is how we grow. Individuals who are transilient know this. Being reflective is our shaping tool that propels us toward a higher consciousness. As Carl Sandburg said, "A man must find time for himself. Time is what we spend our lives with. If we are not careful, we find others spending it for us.... It is necessary now and then for a man to go away by himself and experience loneliness; to sit on a rock in the forest and ask of himself, 'Who am I, and where have I been and where am I going?'"[2] To sustain momentum in life we need to be reflective. In this ironic statement, Soren Kierkegaard, said, "Life can only be understood backwards; but it must be lived forwards."[3]

The seventh and final transilient quality is finding a mission or purpose. Aimlessness exacerbates the aging process because there is significant stress in trying to ascertain why you're here and where you are going. Individuals without a purpose become dependent on others

---

1

2

3

for direction. They shift courses willy-nilly and tend to be swept up by the strongest winds. They are gamblers with time, who rely on luck and the direction of the wind. Those who have a mission or purpose are focused and make decisions that are shaped by their goals. They are flexible enough to change when necessary, but they "keep their eye on the prize."[4] They are doing more than just passing through life; they are motivated by a larger vision. Viktor E. Frankl in his book, *Man Searches for Meaning,* expresses, "In some way, suffering ceases to be suffering at the moment it finds meaning."[5] This change in perspective gives us resiliency and excitement about living.

In the following seven chapters, each of the seven transilient traits will be illustrated by a case study of a client that came in for treatment. Each client had one of these transilient qualities. In the second section of each chapter, these attributes will be given detailed consideration by highlighting the lives of seven prominent personalities who had these same transilent qualities.

4

5

Table of Contents

Part Two – The Tools

Part One

Seven Transilient Qualities

Chapter One
Connecting with Nature

"Haley. Haley, stop!" her mother yelled. Haley and her mother tumbled into my office. The mother lunged forward trying to take something out of her daughter's hand. She had taken something from the waiting room and her mother insisted Haley put it back.

"Let's not worry about that right now," I said. "Have a seat both of you and we'll deal with it later. How can I help you?"

"Last week I went to parent teacher conferences," her mother explained. "Haley's teacher suggested that I have her tested for ADD (Attention Deficit Disorder). Her teacher recommended you and I was glad that we could get in to see you so soon."

While her mother explained, Haley touched everything in my office. I had Montessori boxes filled with geometric puzzles. In record time, she had all the puzzle pieces spilled on the floor. I sat calmly with her on the floor, helping her put the pieces back in the boxes. I was systematic and directive and Haley had good self-control. As soon as I turned to talk to her mother, her attention would divert, and I would have to say something to her to get her attention back.

I made a mental note of that behavior because it had observational merit. Children's behavior is quite transparent and telling.

"Well, the first step in this assessment process is to do a parent interview," I said. "This interview gives me insight into what is bringing the two of you in to see me. It is best if Haley stays in the waiting room so you and I can talk privately. It's easier to share information when it's just the two of us. I think we can make this work. I'll have one of my secretaries watch Haley in the waiting room."

Haley reluctantly went out, mostly concerned about what her mother was going to say about her. She found a pop-up book to read but gave me a bewildered glare as I opened the waiting room door.

I pointed to the clock and said, "Your mother will be out when the long hand is on ten." I got the attention of one of the secretaries and pointed to Haley. The secretary figured out the signal. As I opened my office to begin the interview, I found Delores, Haley's mother, frazzled.

"She is such a handful. Her brother Sid is not like that at all. I don't know what I'm doing wrong."

"Well, it will help if we get her background." I said as I gathered the Developmental History forms. Haley was nine years old and the oldest in the family. Her brother was two years younger and the "apple of his mother's eye." Haley showed signs of jealously early on, and at one point dropped a handful of sand on him while he was sleeping in his crib.

"Ever since that happened, I don't trust her with him," Delores confessed. "They seem to get along better now, but that behavior just haunts me."

I continued with the questions that were on the Parent Interview form, and found her early development to be unremarkable. However, something that did stand out was her love for the outdoors. Delores described her as one who would collect rocks, leaves, toads, and, sometimes, even snakes. Haley spent hours outside after school in the woods behind their house. She would search out woodland animals and track deer. She knew how many squirrels were in the neighborhood and where they lived. Just the other day, Delores saw Haley become mesmerized by a colony of ants. Her mother noticed that Haley had complete focus on those ants for about an hour.

"Her hands are always moving," her mother, lamented. "She's such a tomboy."

She told me Haley and her dad would play baseball in the backyard after he got home from work. They would play until the sun went down, and they would get just filthy. Up until just recently, she had done well in school.

The next piece of information Delores shared was the most telling. Delores's husband, Roger had filed for a divorce in the past month because of an extramarital affair that he had, so he moved out of the house less than a week prior. Delores was devastated and sobbed when she shared this information.

Haley is not only losing her father, she is losing a friend. I thought. *So much of my practice has been dealing with young children and, clinically, I know this is a huge disruption for Haley. Also, anxiety is the last route to Attention Deficit Disorder. The brain can only handle so much turmoil and then the frontal lobes cease to function properly. I suspect Haley's teacher saw dramatic behavior changes shortly after her father filed for divorce, and that the distracted behavior increased when her father was packing his things to leave the house.*

"Well," I said after the interview. "I think testing is in order. Let's schedule a three-hour block of time that will work for all of us."

I knew Haley's scattered behavior would be difficult for me, so I scheduled a lunchtime break in between the three hours. This would be beneficial for both Haley and myself.

When the testing day came, Haley was suffering with a cold, so that slowed her down. She seemed to revive after she became involved with the testing. The first assessment was the IQ test, which measured natural aptitude. The second was an achievement test which measured how much has been learned. The third one was the TOVA (Test of Variables of Attention) test, which is a machine test used to determine her distractibility when given visual stimuli. This test measured the different components of attention and self-control. Those components are variability (consistency), response time (speed), commission errors (impulsivity), and omissions, which determine focus and vigilance. If the first two tests show signs of an attention problem, then the TOVA played a key role in the certainty of the diagnosis.

Surprisingly, Haley handled the testing very well and I thought she enjoyed the one on one attention. The results were clear. She had ADD with hyperactivity (ADHD). The next step was outlining a treatment plan.

The usual treatment for this diagnosis called for medication and behavioral retraining. I set up an appointment with a psychiatrist, so he could prescribe the best medication for Haley. Behavioral retraining was another part of the treatment plan.

Next, the relationship between Delores and Haley needed work and I recommended that Delores come in separately for treatment. When she came in for her appointment, I used *Barkley's Parent Training Program* to improve their relationship. This is one of the most effective methods I used in my practice. The procedure necessitated that Delores initiate twenty minutes of special time each day or at least four or five times per week.

Most importantly, Haley needed to choose the activity. With this method, for once the child is in control. The mother was not to critique her daughter, but instead, point out the positives of what she did. The prevailing sentiment was one of appreciation and acceptance of her daughter during the time. Statements like, "I like it when we play quietly like this," or "You are so creative to be able to find a way to solve these difficult problems" reinforced what took place. Those affirmations helped promote a tight bond between the two, all meant to "fill up Haley's cup."

The outcome was wonderful. Haley and her mother became close and respectful of each other. Haley needed more than medication and a better relationship with her family.

The last part of the treatment plan was to find a more suitable educational set-up for Haley. Hands-on activities were clearly her style of learning. Summer school, which was just around the corner, offered classes in geology and rock formations. Participation in this program was recommended, along with the Zoo School in the fall. Part of the local zoo, the curriculum was almost completely hands-on. Her teacher, mother, and I collaborated in our efforts to get her a placement there for the following fall and we were successful.

That fall, Haley and Delores came in for a follow up session, and Haley was doing very well in the Zoo School.

"I love taking care of the animals and I'm the only girl that handles the snakes," she said with a delightful smile. "School is fun for me."

Happily, not only was her educational life on track, but her relationship with her mother was much better as well. Her father was part of her life, too, since they both enjoyed sports and they found time to do sports together. She was still on medication, but we decided that she should come in every six months to determine if further medication would be necessary.

In October of that year, a friend and I decided to go to the local zoo, since they were having a special show with the animals that Saturday. To my surprise, Haley was in the snake exhibit holding a snake. She let some of the participants handle the snakes. With a wide smile, she beamed with pride. Just six short months previously, she had been desperately struggling to stay above water.

Haley finally found her "transilience connection." Before therapy ended, she talked about how she wanted to establish a nature center, so other children could experience the joys of taking care of animals. She became a shining example of people who have become successful by connecting with nature and by embracing their unique learning style.

Teddy Roosevelt
"Keep your eyes on the stars, and your feet on the ground."
– Teddy Roosevelt

Another shining example of healing through nature comes from the life of the twenty-sixth President of the United States, Teddy Roosevelt. A severe asthmatic as a child, who at times experienced asthma attacks, that were so severe he feared smothering to death.

He confronted this malady head-on by embracing an extremely rigorous outdoors lifestyle. While hiking with his family in the Alps, he discovered that he could keep pace with his father. What surprised him was that physical exertion actually minimized his asthma and made him feel better. On one of the camping trips he was pummeled by two

7

older boys. He chose not to live in fear. True to form, this prompted him to find a boxing coach who could teach him how to box successfully. While at Harvard, Teddy participated in the sports of rowing and boxing. He was runner-up in a Harvard boxing tournament. Spurred on by his remarkable father, he became a strong, vigorous young man. Yet, as sometimes happens, tragedy struck, not once but three times.

In February of 1878, his beloved father died when he was twenty years old. The words his father spoke to him just before Teddy left for Harvard were gems of wisdom that he cherished, "Take care of your morals first, your health next and, finally, your studies." He followed his father's advice to the end of his life and this was also characteristic of him during his presidency.

Two years later, when Teddy was twenty-two, he married Alice Hathaway Lee. They were happily married for four years when Alice died suddenly just two days after delivering their first child, also named Alice. Sorrow heaped upon sorrow when Teddy's mother Mittie died of typhoid fever just one day before he lost his wife. Overwhelmed and disheartened, he said, "The light has gone out of my life." He put baby Alice in the care of his sister, Bamie, in New York City and spent three years grieving his losses. He resumed custody of Alice three years later.

Three huge losses very close together would crush most men, but it was at this time that his love of nature was manifested. He vigorously connected with nature by moving to North Dakota. There, he took on the challenges of the rugged outdoor life. He learned to ride western style, roped cattle, became a wilderness hunter, and wrote three books about his adventures. He established his first ranch,

"Chimney Butte Ranch" on the banks of the Little Missouri River and, later, a second ranch, "Elk Horn" just north of Medora, North Dakota. He rose above his circumstances by taking on more and more physical challenges. Nature was his teacher and his healer. Quite significantly, he garnered the respect of the native Dakota cowboys.

A spiritual strength happens when man and nature connect. As Rachel Carson says in *Silent Spring*,[1] "Those who contemplate the beauty of the earth find reserves of strength that will endure as long as life lasts." This is also true for Richard Louv who, in his landmark book, *Last Child in the Woods: Saving our Children from Nature Deficit Disorder*[2] began an international conversation about the relationship between children and nature. His vision for a better world is when children become as immersed in nature as they are in technology. In this book, Louv summarizes three frontiers that further explain our current conundrum.

The first frontier discussed was the Lewis and Clark era, which largely occurred during the 1800s. This was a time of land awareness and acquisition. It was a time filled with expeditions and topographical discoveries. Americans were awed by the amount and variety of land in the frontier. Imagining the wilderness captured the thoughts and dreams of the many adventurers. These expeditions opened the way for the "Westward Ho" movement. So many Americans desired to own land.

The second frontier was the utilitarian land use and its preservation. This was the Teddy Roosevelt era of the 1900s. He ran as William McKinley's Vice President and,

---

1

2

Kathryn Den Houter Ph.D.

when McKinley died in office, he rose to the office of President on September 14, 1901 and held office until March 4, 1909. Teddy saw himself as a frontier explorer. In 1905, at his Inauguration as President, cowboys on horseback rode down Pennsylvania Avenue with the Seventh Calvary on parade. Even the American Indians joined in the celebration. It was at this same time the American family was completely dependent on the land for their living. Nature played a key role in their daily routines, and in their ultimate survival.

The third frontier is what we have today. This is a time when nature is only a secondary part of our lives. When Louv asked a fourth grader in California where he would most like to play, indoors or outdoors, this was his answer: "I like to play indoors better, 'cause that's where all the electric outlets are." My, how times have changed! According to Louv, natural play is being squeezed out by regulations, needing building permits to build a tree house, threats of lawsuits, fears of disrupting habitats of endangered species, homeowners' association rules, overdevelopment of land, and a distrust of what might be lurking in the dark woods (is that where the boogeyman lives?). When Louv was a youngster, he saw himself as nature's frontiersman, much like Teddy Roosevelt. He goes on to say, "The woods were my Ritalin. Nature calmed me, focused me, and yet excited my senses."

Louv defines nature as bio-diverse and forever abundant—related by loose parts, but most of all, nature enhances our capacity for wonder. When Teddy Roosevelt connected with nature, he was renewed, healed and his capacity for wonder was restored. He rose above his circumstances and became transilient.

Study Questions
Connecting with Nature

These questions have been carefully crafted to help you get to your transilient self. Answer them the best you can if you are working alone. If you have the support of a group, so much the better, since these questions are designed for group discussion.

1. What transilient quality did Haley and Teddy Roosevelt have in common?

2. How did this quality help them transcend their difficulties?

3. How did this make them resilient (strong, durable)?

4. How would you describe your connection with nature?

5. What are some behaviors (3-5) that you will change or add to become closer to nature?

Chapter Two
What's Around the Corner?

Grandma Mary—Mary Elizabeth actually, but we called her Grandma Mary—had joined my Grief Recovery Group and attended regularly every week for three months. It was a term of endearment, because most of the group members were one or two decades younger than the eighty-two year–old Mary.

She was quite outspoken and insisted on giving advice to other group members, a force to be reckoned with, and she made us laugh. "Slow down, Grandma Mary. I want you to listen to the other group members," I would suggest. Try doing some active listening." That didn't stop her comments, however, and she continued to share her opinions regularly in the group.

At the start of one of the group sessions, I announced that I was moving to another firm to continue my psychological practice there. I did express some trepidation about the move, but encouraged everyone to stay in the group. I assured them that this group would continue at the new clinic.

"Don't ever be afraid to start over!" Grandma Mary said, flashing a radiant smile. Her dark eyes twinkled because she knew she was giving advice again and it was to *me*, her counselor. I valued her comment because it was typical of her very wise pronouncements.

Valentine's Day happened to be on one of the group nights, so stories of Valentine mishaps were shared. One group member laughed when she told us that she wished her unattached friends a "Happy Independence Day" rather than "Happy Valentine's Day." Another group member said he had an engagement ring for sale that was worn by the devil.

Grandma Mary listened to his tales of woe and said firmly, "DNRR!" We all looked at her, wondering what she meant. "Do Not Resuscitate Romance," she said with a glimmer in her eye. Another group member told us about a time when her then boyfriend asked her over for a seven-course meal. Intrigued with his cooking skills, she took him up on the offer. It turned out to be a hot dog and a six-pack. "DNRR!" was Grandma Mary's quick retort.

It was a privilege to get to know her. She signed up for the group because she had recently lost her second husband, someone with whom she shared a deep love. The loss was huge and she didn't know how to begin the grieving process. She became immobilized with depression. Her past nine months were filled with misery and the loss was still raw. Her neighbor suggested that she find a grief recovery group, so she contacted my office.

When she shared her story, it was clear that she was processing the loss of her first husband, also. It is not uncommon to set off even deeper grief when there is unfinished grieving from a previous loss. In spite of this sorrow, she was able to rise above some very difficult traumas.

Her first husband died tragically from a farming accident. While repairing his tractor out in the field, his coveralls got caught in the power takeoff and the tractor pulled him in and ground him into the machinery. Mary found Herbert dead in the field when she took out his lunch. Lunch with him in the field was something she enjoyed, so finding him dead, and in that manner, was especially traumatic for her. The loss of her husband and her children's father was huge. The grief hung heavy on her heart. Never would they be grandparents together and never again would they share the joy of farming together. This part of her life was over, a broken dream.

Although she was grief-stricken, she finished raising their youngest son who was in high school, comforted and helped her two older children and handled the daily operations of the farm. This included finding someone to cultivate, plant and harvest her crops. Also, the cows needed milking, the chickens needed to be fed and butchered at the right time.

Her neighbors were helpful, but much of it she had to do herself. Managing the financial books was another big job that fell on her shoulders. She was one tough, resilient lady. For five years, the farming operations went fairly smoothly. In the 1980s, during the farming crisis, she became victim of the downturn in the economy. Bankruptcy was her only option, yet another loss.

Rather than wallowing in the devastation, she started over. With very little money in her pocket, she moved to town and found a job managing an apartment complex and was given an apartment with free rent in exchange. To bring in some income, she worked at the local Dairy Queen. This was seasonal work, so, during the winter months, she cleaned houses. She managed quite well.

One summer's day, she met a gentleman while working at the Dairy Queen. Tom was a bit younger than she was, but shared her ability to adapt and change. They laughed a lot, talked about some of the adventures they wanted to experience, and decided they wanted to be together.

Following a short courtship, they married and became a couple. It was a time of lightness, love, and laughter for them. Over the years, they discovered treasures in each other and found fantastic finds on their journeys. They were quite a team! "Isn't life surprising?" she said with a satisfied sigh.

At the group sessions, she reminisced about those adventurous times she had with her second husband. He encouraged her to write poetry, which she did in full measure. She encouraged him to pursue his family's genealogy. They traveled and camped at most of the National Parks in the United States. They continued to inspire each other as well as their children and grandchildren. She trusted that God wanted the best for her, so that, along with her openness to life, made her truly transilient. She was always ready for a new experience.

Sadly, her second husband had diabetes and was on dialysis the last two years of his life. He became weaker and weaker until, one day, his heart just stopped. Their thirty years marriage stopped also. Grandma Mary missed his companionship and, most of all, being able to love and care for someone. For a while, life stopped for her, but through her efforts and the help of the grief recovery group, she was able to find new dreams to give meaning to her life again. She even thought she might serve in the Peace Corp.

The group ended after six months and we all said our goodbyes. So much growth happened for all of us! I still think about Grandma Mary and wonder where she is and if, perchance, she has found another friend to share her love and dreams. God bless her.

Most of all, I will never forget Grandma Mary's two

pronouncements: "Don't ever be afraid to start over" and "Isn't life surprising?" Her life was free from fear, because she was always anticipating the next chapter. Her forward momentum gave her life excitement. She lived in eager anticipation wondering,

"What's around the corner?"

Maria Montessori

All people are made happy through meaningful work.

"Well-behaved women seldom make history." This 1976 quote by Laurel Thatcher Ulrich[1] epitomizes the life of Maria Montessori. A female born in 1896 in Italy had an uphill battle just to gain credibility. This was during the time of Freud and repression and the Victorian Era, which emphasized form over substance. These enemies of freedom and self-expression were no match for Maria, a fighter at every turn. Her determination combined with her inquisitive nature pushed her to discover "what's around the corner."[2]

After graduating from Secondary school, she decided to go to the University of Rome to study medicine. Her father pleaded with her to take a more acceptable path for a woman. She refused. During her initial interview with the university's clinical director, Guido Boccelli cautioned her to find a more appropriate place for a woman, but she was determined to enter a man's world and excel.

In spite of these obstacles, Maria became the first woman doctor in Italy. It came at a cost, since she bore the brunt of much hostility and was harassed and teased by her male classmates. During this time at the university, it was considered improper and even scandalous for a female to dissect the naked body of a cadaver in the same room as her male counterparts. Her professor ordered her to do the dissections alone in the evening after class. The smell of formaldehyde from the cadavers was so toxic and putrid that she took up smoking to cover the stench.

1
2

She persisted and even won an academic prize during her first year in medical school. Because she proved herself, she was given an assistantship at the local hospital. It was this opportunity that generated a remarkable career. "No matter what life throws my way, I will rise above it," her inner voice shouted. [3]

While at this hospital, Maria had a love affair with Giuseppe Montesano, the co-director of the Orthophrenic School that employed her. The result of this relationship was her son, Mario Montessori. He was born on March 31, 1898. She had to keep Mario's birth a secret for, if it was exposed, she would have to give up her career, since women in Italy were not allowed to have children and a career at the same time. Giuseppe and Maria had an agreement that they would not marry anyone else. For two years, Maria hid Mario in a foster care home outside the city. Unfortunately, Giuseppe broke his promise, fell in love with another woman, and married her. Maria, reeling from this betrayal, became even more focused on her career. She rose above her circumstance, gained momentum to complete her goals, and this transilient quality gave her strength. Maria once said, "All people are made happy through meaningful work." That was true for her as well. From the position of a humble assistant, she was inspired to research and develop a method of education that is revolutionary even today.

In her work with mentally retarded children, she watched how children naturally learned. She spent hours and hours observing them and writing copious notes. From this research, she designed didactic equipment that integrated the five senses. Out of these observations came four curricula

3

that children need for intellectual development; practical life, sensorial input, language skills, and mathematics lessons.

Practical life included daily routines such as pouring, washing dishes, and using kitchen utensils among other skills. The sensorial area included shape, color, sound, and texture-matching activities. The language area involved nomenclature, the three period lesson emphasized labeling, recognition and recall of objects in the environment. Finally, the mathematics area focused on symbol and quantity association, skip counting with beads and a sensorial approach to algebraic equations.

According to her, natural learning started from the concrete and moved toward the abstract. Classroom curricula progressed from the known to the unknown. Visual activities moved from the left to the right to get children ready for reading. These findings have been assimilated into educational materials and methods today.

For eighteen of my twenty years of teaching, I used the Montessori Method. As a Montessori directress, I saw remarkable developmental gains in my students. Each and every day, as I used the Montessori curriculum, it spotlighted the genius of Maria Montessori. By engaging children in captivating learning activities on their level, a spontaneous discipline developed within them.

The job of the directress is to observe the child, take notes, and then, find the match between the child and the environment. This connection is critical. During her era, so much of education was the teacher lecturing and "spoon-feeding" students. Her method proved revolutionary because it relied on the child's inner desire to learn.

Kathryn Den Houter Ph.D.

Maria Montessori's spiritual nature was demonstrated by her view of the child. She saw them as unique creations from God. The child, from her perspective, had an inner-drive to learn about God and his creation. Colorful and attractive didactic materials were placed in the classrooms and children had the freedom to choose their activity and to be engrossed in the activity as long as they wanted. The result was children who were at peace because they were not hurried by external schedules. Education for Montessori children became inwardly directed rather than directed by others.

In the 1930s, when Mussolini established his dictatorship in Italy, the Montessori Method lost favor. Her philosophy was to give children choices in the classroom. This ran counter to the autocratic ideology of his regime. It was considered too democratic and not compatible with "El Duce's" totalitarian state. Maria was asked to leave Italy, her homeland.

She left Italy, but this just fortified her resolve. She started new schools in the Netherlands and in India. Her "Casa de Bambini" (Children's House) celebrated widespread acceptance. Alexander Graham Bell endorsed her method, which resulted in the establishment of over two-hundred Children's Houses in the 1930s, '40s, and '50s in the United States.

Having lived through WWII, Maria, particularly concerned about how to create a lasting peace in the world, contended that it started in the classroom with "meaningful work." This kind of "work" included learning activities that fulfilled a developmental need within the child. Once the child was "full," they were at peace with themselves. This fulfillment carried over into peace and love among their classmates and then, into their world as adults.

It was her international peace initiatives that gave her acclaim. She was nominated three times for the Nobel Peace Prize (1949, 1950, and 1951). She never received more than a nomination, but she was also awarded the French Legion of Honor, Office of the Order of Orange Nassau, and an Honorary doctorate at the University of Amsterdam.

After a very full, transilient life, she died at the age of 81 in the Netherlands of a cerebral hemorrhage. She began her life filled with gender discrimination and other social barriers, but because of her indomitable spirit, she rose above her circumstance to become the "doctor with a worldwide reputation."

Kathryn Den Houter Ph.D.

Study Questions
What's Around the Corner?

These questions have been carefully crafted to help you get to your transilient self. Answer them the best you can if you are working alone. If you have the support of a group, so much the better, since these questions are designed for group discussion.

1. What transilient quality did Grandma Mary and Maria Montessori have in common?

2. How did this quality help them transcend their difficulties?

3. How did this make them resilient (strong/durable)?

4. Do you have a sense of adventure when you live your life? If so, list examples. If not, list some behaviors that you can do make your life more of an exciting "treasure hunt."

Chapter Three
Dark Walking

One does not become enlightened by imagining figures of light; but, by making the darkness conscious." ~ Carl Jung

"I feel such an ache in the middle of the night." These were the first words out of Sharon's mouth as she talked to me. Counseling took the better part of two years and was for the most part a grueling ordeal. Her grief was like a cement block around her neck.

Sharon was widowed nine months before she came in for therapy. She had a complex grieving process, often referred to as "complicated bereavement" among psychologists. Her marriage had been a difficult one—a love/hate relationship. While her husband was alive, she didn't spend much time dwelling on the deficits of her marriage, but instead tried to make the best of it. "If you have a lemon, you have to make lemonade," she often said ruefully, but that "can-do" attitude didn't afford her any comfort after his death. Sharon kicked herself for not confronting the tough issues in their marriage and even felt guilty for her husband's death. She felt those marriage failures only contributed to the stress he was under at the end of his life.

Harold, Sharon's husband was described as a brilliant-but-moody man, a well-known real estate developer. The recession of 2008 reared its ugly head and, every month, money came up short. Huge investments incurred bigger losses.

Sharon and Harold had three children who were the bright spots in their marriage. They were well cared for and all had promising futures, but college expenses came at a time when Harold's businesses were sinking. In a frantic move, he remortgaged his home so their oldest two children could have money for college. They owned a beautiful, five-bedroom home in the best area of town. Harold wanted nothing but the best for himself and his family. Appearance and "looking the part" was important to him. Sharon had feelings of doom and gloom knowing their assets were dwindling and their future uncertain.

As their solvency vanished, Harold's moods cycled. He went to work every morning trying desperately to manage the financial mess. When he came home, he was explosive, his mood rapidly spiraling downward. Sharon suffered insults, mind-games, bouts of yelling and daily rants from him. She cowered in the face of it. His moods annihilated any of her previous tender feelings. Day by day, she handled the care of the children, now young adults, handled the chores of the household, and spent times with friends who consoled her. In spite of this support, it became harder and harder for her to function.

One morning, Harold felt physically ill and, finally, decided to go to the doctor. Sharon said that he hadn't been to see their doctor in over five years. Though the blood work and routine tests the doctor ordered proved negative, the next day everything came to a crashing halt. Harold came home from work early claiming that he was not feeling well. While walking through the kitchen, he slumped over and collapsed on the floor, felled by a massive heart attack. Sharon, shocked, dropped her cup of coffee on the floor, and started CPR, but he was unresponsive. She tried harder, but to no avail. Fortunately, their youngest son came home and called 9-1-1. The ambulance came quickly. They used a defibrillator, but could not resuscitate him. They rushed him to the hospital where they pronounced him DOA.

What followed for Sharon was, in many ways, worse than the events leading up to his death. In denial about his own inevitable death, Harold had no will. His real estate company, a "house of cards," stood on the brink of collapse. His estate was also a mess.

Sharon had to step up to the plate and deal with some very difficult circumstances. She wanted to keep the house for her children so they could process grief in a familiar place, putting her own grief on hold until his real estate businesses finished bankruptcy proceedings. She hired nine attorneys at different times to get through his financial morass.

Their children, protected from their father's problems, were saddened by their father's financial struggles. Even though they chuckled when they described him as having a "type A" personality, they saw him as successful and competent.

The situation became even worse when her youngest son went off to college. Now all alone in that cavernous house, Sharon had managed to sort out the estate and stood ready to deal with her grief. She had discovered the love/hate relationship they had together in life was plaguing her after Harold's death. She wanted to dwell on the good memories, but the last part of their marriage had been miserable, both of them hanging on by their fingernails.

The dark thoughts about their life together haunted her in the middle of the night. No longer a beautiful home to her, the walls held the darkness of their relationship. During the night, she would hear noise and see shadows that were so frightening that she would be on high alert until the sun rose in the morning so she slept during the day.

Having faced so many obstacles with courage, it was time to confront her fear in the dark, all of it painful. At first the sleeplessness combined with haunting fear in the middle of the night was too much for her to deal with by herself. She tried medication, drinking herself to sleep, yoga and exercising so much that she flopped into bed exhausted, yet none of it could sustain a good night's sleep. That's when she came to see me.

Therapy started slowly because she hesitated to share her married life with me. Perhaps guilt kept it locked-up inside of her or, maybe shame. Once it came out, however, she became more relaxed. Smiles, and even laughter, became part of her disposition. Undertaking the grief was complicated for her because she couldn't find the end of the maze at first. However, once the pain of her marriage trap became conscious, little by little Sharon found freedom. Her spirit rose above her circumstances, and she reclaimed her delightful self. The key was to separate her life from her husband's life. New life patterns emerged and she established future goals. Sharon was free from overwhelming fear, except for her persisting terrors during the night. During one of the last sessions, Sharon came in with a question,

"Have you ever heard of a breath prayer?"

'Yes I have," I replied, "it can be a powerful method of healing. Breathing is referred to often in the Scriptures.[1] This is good for us physically, psychologically and spiritually. When breathing in we can rejuvenate with a healing breath and when we breathe out, we can release our tensions."

"Could you help me find a breath prayer that I can use in the middle of the night when I'm terrified?"

"Do you say anything to yourself, now, that gives you peace?" I asked.

She thought for a moment, "The spiritual glow of my heavenly Father and the light of Christ makes me feel calm."

"Let's shorten that a bit so it fills up one inhale. How about 'I breathe in the light of Christ? Let's try that." We closed our eyes and said together, "I breathe in the light of Christ." We both agreed this would work.

"What do you think would work for the exhale?" I asked.

Sharon took more time to process that question and said, "I think my fear is caused by the devil and he's the opposite of spiritual freedom. I see Jesus as light and the devil as dark."

"Hmmm. How about it if we try this one? I breathe in the light of Christ, and let out the dark side of the devil." Sharon smiled and shook her head "yes," breathed a sigh of relief, and settled into the couch cushions. She agreed to give it a try during the night for a week and see if the terrors would go away.

The next week, she came into my office all smiles, and I could tell from her expression that our approach had been

---

[1]

successful. Her face was more relaxed and she even looked younger.

"Most nights I am able to sleep through the night," she explained. "When I do wake up, I do the breath prayer and I soon fall back to sleep. I have found my way through the last part of the maze." She seemed both confident and comforted by her ability to conquer her fears through the breath prayer.

Transilient people learn how to walk through the dark. They learn to transform the nights of terror by confronting those fears. It is an essential quality for transiliency, because it is about how we handle losses. When fear of night and dark is transformed into light and grace, this translates into true spiritual freedom.

It reminds me of Barbara Taylor's book, *Learning to Walk in the Dark*, which says, "Like darkness itself, the dark night of the soul means different things to different people. Some use the phrase to describe the time following a great loss, while others remember it as the time leading up to a difficult decision. Whatever the circumstances, what the stories have in common is their description of a time when the soul was severely tested, often to the point of losing faith, by circumstances beyond all control. No one chooses the dark night; the dark night *descends*."[2]

---

[2]

Stevland Morris

It's not so much learning how to walk through the dark, but more a matter of trying to make sense of it. Perhaps the "dark" is the fear of the night, or not having vision or direction, or reckoning with the loss of eyesight itself. The transilient individual masters the "dark walk."

It takes courage to look inside your soul and gaze at what lurks there. It's a self-reckoning when you see yourself without props. There are no cell phones, distractions, or entertainment. You are eyeballing *yourself*. Those who do that walk are really saying to themselves that they matter. When the hidden self is discovered and made conscious, inner strength is developed. Then the next step is to integrate that part into your self-image. As your identity becomes complete, you gain a comfort in your own skin. Others feel safe and relaxed around you because peace emanates from you. The journey into the self takes just as much, if not more, courage as the journey into space.

One person who has that bravery is Stevland Hardaway Morris. He was born on May 13, 1950 ... without sight. You might know him by his stage name "Stevie Wonder." Born in Saginaw Michigan, the third of six children, his mother, Lula Mae Hardaway, after divorcing his father, Calvin, moved her family to Detroit, Michigan to be closer to her family. He was born six weeks prematurely and, because of that, he developed ROP (retinopathy of prematurity). With this condition, the eyes stop growing, causing the retinas to detach.

Stevie began playing musical instruments early. He had a love affair with all of them: the piano, the harmonica, and the drums. He formed a singing partnership with a friend and they called themselves, "Stevie and John." They played on street corners, and occasionally at parties and dances.

Stevie Wonder is considered one of the most creative and most respected musical performers of our time. Blindness at birth required him to self-reckon. He was quoted as saying, "Many years ago, there were those who said, 'Well, you have three strikes against you: you're black, you're blind and you're poor,' but God said to me, 'I will make you rich in the spirit of inspiration, to inspire others as well as create music to encourage the world to a place of oneness and hope and positivity.' I believed Him and not them."

As suggested in his song, "Have a Talk with God," faith plays a major part in his life. He repeats this phrase, "When you feel your life's too hard, just go have a talk with God."

He attributes his stardom to the ability and the opportunity that God gave him. Certainly, his handicap would have been unbearable without this inner strength.

Stevie Wonder is a devout Christian who got his start by singing at the Whitestone Baptist Church in Detroit, Michigan. In the 1970s, he practiced Transcendental Meditation with his first wife, Syreeta Wright, a Motown singer and songwriter. As Stevie says in a book by James Haskins, titled *The Story of Stevie Wonder,*[3] "Much of life is about the choices we make. We all have that ability. The difference is how we use it." Stevie Wonder has been able to transcend his circumstances. Within that world of darkness, Stevie Wonder has been able to know what is important and what he needs to do to thrive.

Tragedy struck on August 6, 1973 when he suffered a serious car accident. In a coma for four days, this resulted in a partial loss in his sense of smell and a temporary loss of taste. Once he regained his health, he performed on stage at Madison Square Garden and purposely chose upbeat, triumphant music to inspire his audience. His transilent qualities were reflected in that performance, and he soared to even greater musical heights. He has won twenty-five Grammys, which is more than any other solo artist. He is in the Rock and Roll and Songwriters Halls of Fame. In 1984 his song, "I Just Called to Say I Love You," was chosen the best original song.

"Sometimes I think I would love just to see the beauty of flowers and trees and birds and the earth and grass," he once said. "Being as I've never seen, I don't know what it's like to see. So in a sense I'm complete. Maybe I'd be

---

[3]

incomplete if I did see. Maybe I'd see some things that I don't want to see, the beauty of the earth compared to the destruction of man. You see, it's one thing when you are blind from birth, and you don't know what it's like to see, anyway. The sensation of seeing is not one that I have and not one that I worry about. "

He announced, however, that he was pursuing an intraocular retinal prosthesis to partially restore his sight. Even though he has reconciled with his blindness and has overcome the stigma and limitations of it, he has a curiosity about what the seeing world is about.

The "dark" is unique for each one of us. It could be the fear of being alone, the fear of the shadows of the nights, fear of the evil that lurks within us, fear of oppression, or loss of control. It is manifested in any number of ways.

Managing the dark is part of our life's work, since it needs to be confronted to avoid being consumed by the fear of it. For Stevie Wonder, coming to terms with his blindness was pivotal in the choices that he made. He chose to focus on what God said to him rather than on what was said by those around him. He was convinced that he was given this musical talent to help the world and to inspire others. He chose to make this world a better place. The other choice would have been to listen to those around him, "You are black, blind, and poor." He changed those words to "I am worthy, talented, and rich in imagination." He cultivated an inspiring mission, and this catapulted him into stardom.

Study Questions
Dark Walking

These questions have been carefully crafted to help you get to your resilient self. Answer them the best you can if you are working alone. If you have the support of a group, so much the better, since these questions are designed for group discussion.

1. What resilient quality did Sharon and Stevie Wonder have in common?

2. How did this quality help them transcend their difficulties?

3. How did that make them resilient (strong/durable)?

4. Do you have a fear of the dark and/or your unconscious self? If so, list behaviors that you can do to make your life less fearful of the dark. If not, briefly explain how you have overcome those fears.

Chapter Four
Overcoming Scarcity with Creativity

Where does creativity fit into the personality of resilient individuals? While listening to a presentation on overcoming scarcity with creativity, I acknowledged the absolute significance of being creative when confronted with life's upheavals. It was at this time that I had an epiphany.

Ah, yes, I thought, *this quality was clearly present in my most resilient clients. The clients who were successful in spite of difficult lives have been creative. Their thought processes were resourceful, and not reactive. Instead, they became proactive and forward thinking as they tackled life's most difficult challenges.*

Family stories of the Depression Era came to mind, a time in our country when everything was scarce. Women made woolen quilts with scraps from old worn out men's suits. They made braided rugs from clothes that were thrown in the ragbag such as old coats and Sunday suits. People saved every scrap and piece of old clothing to use. My grandma used old silk stockings to stuff pillows.

Gardening was more than a hobby, since vegetable gardens were essential for survival. Holes in the soles of shoes were remedied by inserting pieces of cardboard inside the shoe. Lovely dresses were made from feed sacks. If you couldn't afford a belt to keep your pants up, a piece of clothesline rope would do. People survived because they were inventive and creative in spite of their shortfalls. This attribute is indispensable today since survival strategies in our world are in short supply. Thinking creatively to solve complex problems today is in even more of a demand.

Two of my clients with this quality come to mind. Both were mothers who were raising two sons by themselves. For sure, there were many differences between Dee and Cheryl, but the spiritual aspects of their journeys were quite similar: joy was depleted due to marital tragedies. One lost her husband due to his infidelity, and the other due to his mental illness. With a broken home and broken dreams, these women had to be creative in the face of huge losses.

The plight of the single mother encompasses scarcity and suffering. First of all, there isn't much money when the main breadwinner abandons the family. Also, there is the heartbreak of broken dreams and family dysfunction caused by pre and post-divorce struggles. Having two sons is mighty challenging for intact families, but even harder for single mothers, since these families have no male role models. However, like so many challenges in life, when done successfully, the rewards are great. Dee and Cheryl were always trying to determine how to help their sons. They wanted them to respect women without being dependent on them. They wanted their sons to be assertive, but NOT overly aggressive or angry. Most important, they didn't want their boys to be singled out or to be picked on by others boys or men. In short, their fathers simply were not around to provide role models when they needed them. Boys want to learn how to be brave and strong in a man's world and it is in the day-to-day tussle and bustle that sons need their fathers. With them not in the picture, the mothers had to learn to run their own households. Often these moms would second-guess themselves, because they had never lived as men. They had to stretch themselves to understand what it meant to grow up male in our society. Dee and Cheryl had to put themselves in their sons' shoes to determine what they needed emotionally, spiritually, and physically. They did double duty by being both mom *and* dad. This forced them to become creative in the face of this scarcity.

Dee and Cheryl sought the advice of therapists for support. Their sons needed counseling, too, especially during their growing up years. Interestingly, they chose to see a female counselor because they weren't comfortable talking with male counselors. Men seemed unfamiliar and different, and they found adult males unreliable and untrustworthy.

Faith and church attendance played a big part with both families. Dee and Cheryl opted not to remarry, because getting their sons launched took all their time and energy. Fortunately, they jumped the hurdles they needed to raise their boys and they did an admirable job. By all standards, they were successful parents. That transilient quality of being creative in the face of scarcity characterized their parenting style.

At the time of the divorces, neither Dee, nor Cheryl, had sufficient money to raise two boys. They developed budgets that were so tight they squeaked. Dee had to go back to college to get a teaching endorsement. Cheryl moved back to her hometown to be near her extended family. All of these transitions required planning, "elbow grease" and, most of all, funds. Dee successfully completed her college training and began teaching. Her teaching job gave her family health insurance, a roof over their heads, and food on the table.

Another expense was instruments and music lessons because both of her sons were musically inclined. One son was introverted and immersed himself in computer games. The other was extroverted and enjoyed school activities.

Dee worked hard and provided everything she could for her boys. Unfortunately, the strain of life took its toll and depression set in for Dee when her oldest son, after graduating from high school, went to college and faltered. He did poorly in his classes, and was fired from several jobs. Confused, he spent years trying to understand the reasons for his parent's divorce and was angry with his mother. They both came back into therapy. Dee's previous efforts paid off again, since her insurance was able to pay for her son's therapy. He did the work he needed to do, began developing successful relationships, and started a career in computers. Dee managed her depression through counseling and was relieved when her oldest son recognized that blaming her for the divorce was misguided. Her youngest son was able to find his career path and continue to develop meaningful relationships. Presently, Dee's family is doing very well.

Cheryl found a job with a major company. The job paid well and she enjoyed stable employment with insurance for her family. Practical and good with a dollar, she saved her money so her two sons could have music lessons and tutoring when they needed help in school. The three of them had weekly Bible sessions, where they learned Bible stories and discussed moral issues. This weekly forum helped them deal with day-to-day school issues. Her boys were introverted, and they confined themselves to the safety of their home. This frustrated her, but she found a creative way to solve this problem. During her vacation time from work, she took her two sons and traveled all over the United States, camping in the National Parks. When they camped, they met other families that were traversing the nation as well. They hiked, camped, fished, and traveled their way to manhood. They learned to work as a team and to solve problems as they tramped through the woods and walked the trails.

Once again, because there was no male role model, the transition from home to the world of college and work was difficult for the oldest son. He failed his college classes and was intimidated by the world of work. After a period of time in counseling, he decided on the military life. This was a good choice for him and he continues to enjoy this career to this day. Cheryl and her younger son decided to go to college together and they are motivating each other. Cheryl is taking on the challenge of college and her son is on track to become a science professional.

My hat goes off to these women because they had to suffer through the loss of a family dream and had to stand tall in the face of this tragedy to find the patience and the gumption to raise their sons creatively. Each day they had to be resourceful and disciplined to meet problems head-on. All this hard work paid off, because their sons are productive members of our society. They have made the transition from boys to men. With their transilience, they were able to rise above their circumstances.

Abraham Lincoln

If ever a person lived who demonstrated overcoming scarcity with creativity, it was Abraham Lincoln. Admirers through the ages have marveled at how much he overcame. He beat the odds. It often happens to those who, though perhaps not as famous as Abraham Lincoln, are transilient. That particular blend of resilience and transcendence occurred in the 1800s with our sixteenth president.

The tragedies he endured included huge personal losses, health issues, financial hardships and numerous political defeats. These personal losses started early when he was just nine years of age when he lost his mother, Nancy. He lost his sister Sarah when she was giving birth to a stillborn son.

He was deeply saddened by this loss because Sarah was his mother substitute. Seven years later, in 1835, Lincoln lost his sweetheart, Ann Rutledge, to typhoid fever. Nevertheless, he found the inner strength to persevere.

His stepmother, Sally, liked Abe, but she acknowledged that he wasn't fond of physical labor. However, he loved to read. He read the classics, philosophy, wrote poetry, and did arithmetic. Occasionally, he received training from itinerant teachers, but the bulk of his education came from a desire to learn and to rise above his circumstances. In spite of these early losses, he became largely self-educated.

Frontier living was harsh. The prairie trails were littered with the bones of those overcome by the elements. If you needed clothes, you sewed them yourself, everything was homemade. If you wanted to eat, you foraged wild berries, hunted game, and cultivated crops. Only the resourceful survived. Scarcity was pervasive.

At the age of twenty-two, Lincoln and two of his relatives agreed to take a load of cargo down the Sangamon River to New Orleans for a local businessman.[1] First, they had to build a boat and make it "river worthy." Once completed, they departed downriver. Misadventure was just around the bend when they were run aground by a milldam. The boat was stuck and about ready to capsize when Lincoln hatched a plan.

"Unload the boat except for the barrels!" he shouted. "Roll the barrels forward." They bore a hole in the front of the boat to let the water out and the boat slid off the dam. They were elated! The owner of the boat was so pleased, he

---
[1]

publically announced that he would build a new boat while they were gone and let Lincoln be her captain.

From this experience, Lincoln developed a fascination with boats. He is the only president with a patent on record. On May 22, 1849, he received a patent (number 6469) for a device that lifted boats over shoals. No doubt, the inspiration of this invention came from his time on the Sangamon and Mississippi Rivers taking cargo to New Orleans.

Henry Whitney, an attorney with whom Lincoln would ride the law circuit,[2] said that when they stopped at a farmhouse for dinner, he would hunt up some machinery and analyze its effectiveness, and at one point said, "Man is not the only animal who labors; but he is the only one who improves his workmanship."

The way Lincoln learned was truly unique. William Herndon, his law partner shared an office with him. One of his mannerisms drove William crazy. Lincoln would read law cases aloud with no thought of how this was bothering his partner. This, however, helped his comprehension. Reading to himself was probably how he learned to read and to amuse himself. I suspect that he was an "auditory learner," so using the sense of hearing was the best route toward understanding. He was even creative in the ways he educated himself. Visualization was another learning technique he used.

How did he get so far in his career as a lawyer and politician? Lincoln might have been very determined, but he also used the psychological technique of visualization.[3] He claimed that if you wanted to be a lawyer, visualize yourself

2

3

as a lawyer and you will be on your way to achieving that dream. He once wrote to a young man who was struggling in school about how his visualization of success might help him as well.

"I know not how to aid you, save in the assurance of one of mature age and much severe experience, that you cannot fail if you resolutely determine that you will not." Lincoln was firmly convinced that if you saw yourself as a success you would create certitude in your mind that would create success.

Lincoln was a patient man and had a deeply spiritual side, both transilient qualities.[4] A close associate, Charles Dana, assistant secretary of war, remembered him as a man who was "… never in a hurry, and who never tried to hurry anybody." Lincoln's inherent patience was due in part to his religious beliefs. On the frontier, preachers debated free will and predestination, a controversy that split churches and denominations. Lincoln favored the predestination doctrine, which formed a framework for his decisions in the affairs of state. Friends believed that this philosophy helped him bear his personal misfortunes as well as the agony of the Civil War. "What is to be will be," Lincoln sometimes stated, "and no cares of ours can arrest nor reverse the decree."

Horace Greeley and others wanted Lincoln to be more dogmatic and authoritative.[5] In one of his newspaper articles, Horace Greeley, called Lincoln "wishy, washy" because, if some new, more convincing information would be revealed, Lincoln would change his mind. This referred to the fact that Lincoln was flexible, especially when more

---

4

5

information was disclosed. At times, he would completely change his position and even break a promise. Once when Lincoln was sitting in a barber's chair, someone chided him.

"Mr. Lincoln, if anybody had told me that in a general crisis like this the people were going out to a little one-horse town to pick out a one-horse lawyer for President, I wouldn't have believed it."[6]

Whirling about in his chair, his face still white with lather, Lincoln responded, "Neither would I, but this is a time when a man with a policy would have been fatal to the country. I have never had a policy; I have simply tried to do what seemed best each day as each day came."

Many have speculated about Lincoln's faith. He attended the Presbyterian Church with his wife and family, but never became a member. He grew up attending the Regular Baptist Church in Kentucky. He was disillusioned by the bitter rivalries he witnessed between denominations in Kentucky, but all of those close to Lincoln saw him as a deeply spiritual man. In his own words, he indicates his respect for the divine.

"That I am not a member of any Christian Church is true, but I have never denied the truth of the Scriptures and I have never spoken with intentional disrespect of religion in general, or of any denominations of Christians in particular."[7]

The horrors of the Civil War were incredibly painful for Lincoln and after fifty thousand American soldiers died in three days, he wrote in his journal, *When I left Springfield I asked the people to pray for me. I was not a Christian. When*

---

[6]

[7]

43

I buried my son, the severest trial of my life, I was not a Christian. But when I went to Gettysburg and saw the graves of thousands of our soldiers, I then and there consecrated myself to Christ. Yes, I do love Jesus."[8]

His life is a testament to truths in the scriptures. He spoke antagonistically toward slavery as being against the teachings of Christianity. Without a doubt, our world is a better place because of him. To the end, he was creative in the face of adversity.

8

Study Questions
Overcoming Scarcity with Creativity

These questions have been carefully crafted to help you get to your transilient self. Answer them the best you can if you are working alone. If you have the support of a group, so much the better, since these questions are designed for group discussion.

1. What do Dee and Cheryl have in common with Abraham Lincoln? Describe in your own words that transilient quality.

2. How did this transilient quality help them overcome their difficulties?

3. How did this quality make them resilient (strong, durable)?

4. Do you consider yourself inventive or creative when in a jam? If so, describe some instances where you have overcome obstacles by thinking creatively. If not, list three behaviors that will help you become more creative when faced with challenges.

Chapter Five
People, People, People

There he sat, across from me, a tall, slender, partially bald sixty-five year old man. His downcast eyes made him look dejected and depressed. He looked neither ugly nor handsome, just ordinary. Sprawled out on the couch, with his legs crossed and arms extended outward across the top of the couch cushions, I started the dialogue by asking how I could be of help.

"I'm not sure" was his reply. Silence followed and I patiently gathered more observations. He did appear depressed, but I wasn't sure. *Maybe testing would help,* I thought. *I could use either the MCMI (Millon Clinical Multiaxial Inventory) or possibly, Burns Depression Checklist.*

"I think testing might help," I said and proceeded to build my case. "An MCMI would give us the most useful information. It is like a snapshot of what is going on right now. One section of the test measures the personality styles and the other part measures the clinical syndromes. The personality styles are longer-standing traits and the clinical syndromes can vary from week to week. What we have found is that the personality style drives the clinical syndromes and we see patterns emerge. These testing results are helpful when developing a treatment plan."

"I don't want to be tested," was his feisty response. "I came to see you because I want to share something with you that not even my wife knows."

"Okay." I said nodding gently.

"I retired a year and a half ago from my career as a high school history teacher. My wife is still working as a science teacher at the same high school. She'll probably retire in two years. I'm not looking forward to that. I have a secret life that she doesn't know about. When she heads off to school in the morning, I head up to the attic and open my secret trunk.

"You have another life that she doesn't know about?" I reflected.

"I do. I feel guilty about it, but I feel driven by my urges. Inside my trunk are beautiful dresses, lingerie, jewelry, hosiery, and high heels. I dress up and sashay around the house, admiring myself in the mirror. I feel complete and calm. I am at peace with myself. You see, I am a woman in a man's body."

What unfolded from that point was a remarkable story of tramsilience. His strength was his ability to connect with helpful people. Joe's mother became pregnant when she was forty-three. His father was a drifter and an alcoholic, so he was raised by a single mother. Joe was born with a cleft lip and palate, so his formative years were spent trying to communicate, first to his mother and, then, to his teachers. Joe described himself as wanting to please them. Once they discerned what he was trying to say, his teachers recognized him as a very bright. He was accepted by his classmates because he was a good athlete. Basketball was his sport and his strength was assisting other players, so he was chosen the MVP his senior year. Because he was a diligent, perceptive student, he kept his grades up and he was accepted into Penn State. For someone who could barely talk, I found all of this quite remarkable.

As a freshman, he made the basketball team and it was during this time a life-altering event happened. One of his teammates had a father who was a doctor, and he knew someone who did pro bono surgeries on cleft palates. Joe made a connection with this doctor and the door of clear communication opened for him. It was exhilarating for him to experience this dramatic change, and he was deeply grateful.

Once the language barrier was removed, his transgender issues became the primary issue. He knew his genitalia were small, so he would hide himself with towels when he showered in the locker rooms. Somehow, he made this work throughout his school career. It became more complicated when he met Jennifer in one of his education classes. They both planned careers in education, and they married after college graduation. His path to an orgasm was quite unique because it only happened when he imagined himself a woman. He never shared these imaginings with Jennifer. In spite of that, they were successful in conceiving two healthy boys, which made Joe deeply grateful.

The relationships he developed with Jennifer and his two sons were exemplary. He described family times filled with deep fondness for each other. Both of his boys wanted Joe to be the best man at their weddings.

"What would happen if they knew who I really am?" he asked me during a session. "I'm afraid to find out because I might lose it all and that would be the worst outcome possible. I'm willing to suffer rather than hurt them."

"What have you said to your wife?" I said.

"Nothing."

"Have you told anybody?"

"No. I feel so lonely, even though I have people who love me all around. My wife loves me, and my boys love me. When I taught, the students loved me, but I feel so lonely. Something so basic as my sexual difference I can't share with anybody else. They are all invested in me being a certain way and because I love them so much, I am willing to live with this ache so I don't hurt them. I've prayed about this asking God, 'Why has this happened to me? The answer I hear is that it is my cross to bear and that, in spite of this emptiness, I do have an abundant life. I wholeheartedly agree, so I always come back to a deep sense of gratitude."

This is when he talked about his mother who had died ten years before. He described her as an unhappy, domineering woman who "hen-pecked" his dad. "I loved my father. He was a gentle, kind soul. My mom was harsh and I kept trying to please her but she was never happy. Something happened to Mom when she was pregnant with me. She spent almost a month in the hospital with kidney failure."

"Do you know when that happened in the pregnancy?" I asked.

"I think it was very early."

If that were true, I thought, *then from my understanding of fetal development, the first testosterone wash and the development of the cleft palate both occur during the first trimester of pregnancy. The mother's health problems might have caused the malformation of the palate and probably reduced the effectiveness of the first testosterone wash. This could explain both problems.* [1]

"Well, Joe, I said. For our next session, I want both you and I to do some research. Please find out exactly when your mother was in the hospital during the pregnancy. Also, do some research about fetal development during the first trimester. I will do some research as well. We'll talk about that at the next session."

At the next session, we shared our findings. Sure enough, we both came to the same conclusion. His mother's hospital stay happened in the first three months of the pregnancy. It was during this time that the fetal development was disrupted. The first testosterone wash was either diminished or never happened and the cleft palate resulted. The palate formation and the sexual development are accomplished during the first trimester.

"If Jennifer knew that your sexual identity issues had a physical explanation do you think she would be more understanding?" I asked.

"I don't know," he said.

"Let's send up a test balloon," I said. Try using a fictitious name and run this scenario by her, see how she reacts and then let's talk about it at the next session."

Joe was ebullient the next time I saw him. "When I talked to Jennifer and shared with her the story about Paul, the fictitious name I used, she seemed to understand that this was something that can happen during fetal development, and that nobody was to blame. I feel optimistic about sharing my story with her.

---

[1]

I don't want to lose her because we are both looking forward to retiring together and enjoying our grandchildren. If she could accept my traipsing around in women's clothing once in a while, that would be good enough for me."

Jennifer was sullen and silent for several days after Joe shared his struggles with her. In the final analysis, she was tolerant about Joe's admission. Fortunately, she didn't try to blame him because it happened during fetal development and was out of his control. Ultimately, she accepted Joe's transgender issues. That's where it stood when Joe completed therapy. Joe was such an admirable, transilient person. He was able to transcend his circumstance because he appreciated and connected with people. He knew how to forge healthy relationships because he was a transilient, caring individual.

Franklin Roosevelt

"Something's wrong. Very, very wrong," Eleanor mumbled under her breath as she approached the fishermen in their boat by the dock. "Would you contact Doctor Bennet in Lubec to see if he could come and check on Franklin?" They nodded in assurance as they motored off to the village. The Roosevelt family was vacationing at Campobello, a small Canadian island off the coast of Maine. Granted, those days had been chaotic for the family. Just two weeks earlier, Eleanor had moved five children, a governess, and her mother-in-law into their large home on the island for the summer. As usual, Eleanor "set up camp" while Franklin tied-up some loose ends in Washington, D.C. regarding a Navy scandal. He also had some obligations connected with his new position as president of the Greater New York Council of the Boy Scouts.

Once his Navy commitments were finished, he left New York on the *Sabalo,* a yacht owned by Van Lear Black, a personal acquaintance. They sailed the Atlantic for three days going up the New England coast to Maine, finally arriving at Campobello where Franklin joined his family.

"I feel logy and tired," he told Eleanor, but that never stopped him from living life "large." He was the catalyst for most of the family entertainment. First of all, he wanted to have a fishing expedition for his friend Van Black and the crew of the *Sabalo.* The next day he did just that. He baited the hooks while traversing a narrow plank between the two cockpits of the yacht. At one point, he fell into the cold water of the Bay of Fundy. The next day, the tenth of August, he sailed with Eleanor, his daughter Anna, and sons James and Elliot on the family sailboat, *Vireo.* After the sail, he took his children swimming at their favorite swimming hole, and raced his sons two miles back home. Once there, Franklin became very ill complaining of a sore back, chills, and nausea. He skipped supper and went to bed. The next morning, his symptoms worsened. He had a fever and weakness in his leg, which got progressively worse. Two days later Roosevelt was paralyzed from the waist down.

Doctor Bennet came and soon recommended that Eleanor contact Doctor Keen, a revered surgeon who vacationed near Campobello. He gave Franklin an exhaustive evaluation and concluded that there was a blood clot in his lower back and recommended that they hire a medical masseuse. It was not until they contacted Doctor Samuel A. Levine that he suspected and later confirmed, polio. Four months of various treatments were initiated with

Kathryn Den Houter Ph.D.

minimal to no effect. Roosevelt remained completely paralyzed from the waist down, and was unable to walk without support.

This was a tragic story until Franklin made life choices that defied the odds.[1] His transilience became apparent shortly after the diagnosis. Convinced that warm water would help him get back on his feet, in 1923, he purchased an old houseboat and sailed to Florida with crew and friends on board. People were always around him because they would drop by to sail with Franklin. At one point, he designed a pulley that could lower him into the water for a swim.

He was utterly convinced, in spite of his doctor's diagnosis, that warm water would cure his paralysis. He started hydrotherapy when he visited the mineral springs at Warm Springs, Georgia. Convinced of the benefits of water therapy, he bought a resort at Warm Springs for treatment of people with polio. Franklin lost the use of his legs and two inches off his height, but the emphasis on rebuilding his body made the rest of his body robust and strong and what followed was many years of excellent health. One story of his exceptional strength was that he snagged a two hundred thirty seven pound shark and wrestled with it on his line for two hours.

From 1928 to 1945, there was the "big cover-up." He relied on others to help him walk and to present well in public. He limited the use of a wheelchair to his private residence. Somehow, he was able to convince people that he was getting better. This was necessary if he wanted to run for office again. Franklin perfected the "two-point walk." He

---

[1]

54

would grip the arm of a strong person on his left and support himself with a cane with his right hand. He would thrust one leg forward from the hip and then, the next leg. This is what he did when he successfully addressed the 1928 Democratic National Convention. His speech was so well received that soon afterwards he launched a campaign for governor of New York.[2]

The cover up became more complicated when he entered the world of politics. He choreographed quite a clever way to avoid the press at his arrivals and departures from venues. Often, his staff had his limousine pull into a parking garage and the railings would be covered-up so the camera couldn't see him climbing stairs. He often traveled by train and positioned himself on the rear platform of the last car. His optimism and persuasiveness convinced the American people that he was strong and healthy. The Secret Service actively interrupted when photos were taken of FDR since they were his allies in the cover up. It wasn't until March 1, 1945 (just a month before he died) that he made a comment in public referring to his disability.

"I hope that you will pardon me for this unusual posture of sitting down, but I know you will realize that it makes it a lot easier for me not to have to carry about ten pounds of steel around on the bottom of my legs." One month after this speech, he died unexpectedly at Warm Springs, Georgia on April 12, 1945 of a cerebral hemorrhage. He was surrounded by close friends.

True to form, Franklin's legacy is a tribute to the people he loved. He had tremendous empathy toward the common man, even though he came from privilege. On January 3,

---

[2]

1938, Roosevelt established the March of Dimes. This was a collaborative effort among scientists, volunteers, and educational initiatives to support those with polio. Because he founded the March of Dimes, a dime was chosen to honor him and the first Roosevelt dime was issued in 1946. Today, the March of Dimes has expanded its field of influence by helping prevent premature birth, birth defects, and infant mortality.

Franklin Roosevelt was a deeply spiritual man as attested in a Radio Broadcast on February 23, 1936. "No greater thing could come to our land today than a revival of the spirit of religion, a revival that would sweep through the homes of the Nation and stir the hearts of men and women of all faiths, a reassertion of their belief in God and their dedication of His will for themselves and for their world. I doubt there is any problem—social, political, or economic—that would not melt away before the fire of such a spiritual awakening."

The choices that he made when faced with a devastating handicap were extraordinary. His capacity to connect with people, to lean on them, to garner their respect and to lead them, was impressive. This was his resilient quality. Because this virtue was accompanied by compassion, his transilience made him the President of the common man.

Study Questions
People, People, People

These questions have been carefully crafted to help you get to your transilient self. Answer them the best you can if you are working alone. If you have the support of a group, so much the better, since these questions are designed for group discussion.

1. What do Joe and Franklin Roosevelt have in common? Describe in your own words that transilient quality.

2. How did this transilient quality help them overcome their difficulties?

3. How did this quality make them resilient (strong, durable)?

4. Do you connect with helpful people when faced with obstacles? If so, list some instances when you have done this. If not, indicate three behaviors that will stretch you in this area.

Chapter Six
The Power of Reflection

It started out to be a pretty routine day. Early in the day, I saw two clients for the check-up phase of their treatments, but the next client was anything but routine. Ian was a seventeen year old who was scheduled for a three-hour testing session. First, on the agenda was completing a developmental history with his parents. His mother brought him, so I conducted the interview with her.

Ian was a good student at Forest Hills, which was considered to be the best public high school in the area. His family, by most standards was upper middle class. Mom was a teacher and his dad an engineer at Lear Siegler. Ian wanted to go to the engineering program at the University of Michigan but acceptance rates were low, and he struggled in his English classes. His parents wanted him tested for a learning disability so they could ascertain the next steps.

I began the testing session with Ian. The assessment proceeded without incident until we were half way through the last test, when Ian haltingly said, "Doctor Den Houter, do you have some time after the testing when I could talk with you?" *I wondered what was behind that question.* There was something on his mind that was distracting him while taking the test. I knew it had to be something significant, so I gave him an understanding smile.

"I'll check my schedule when we're done," I said.

The last half hour of the testing seemed to go more quickly. He gained momentum, as if a load had been lifted. With the testing complete, I packed up the testing supplies and checked my calendar for my first available appointment. I had an opening from three to four that afternoon. When I mentioned the time to Ian, he thought that would work because his mother had taken the day off.

I opened the door of the waiting room and called her into my office. "Mrs. Peerent, your son would like another session with me, and he was hoping that it would be sometime today. I told her I had an opening at three. She looked at Ian and then, at me. "Is it something about the testing?" she asked.

"I'm not sure, but I do think it's something important."

She looked at Ian again and said, "Okay, I think we can make that work. We'll go out for lunch and will be back here at three."

My thoughts wandered. *Maybe there are family problems or maybe he has some relationship issues or maybe he doesn't want to go to U of M, but just wants to please his dad.*

I saw my next two clients and waited for Ian. The phone light blinked red, so I knew he was in the waiting room. Following the usual routine, I went to the waiting room door, opened it and found a very nervous young man. I made eye contact with him, and guided him into my office.

"Have a seat, Ian. How can I help you?" I asked.

What followed was an unusually long, silent pregnant pause. *Something must be very painful. The longer the wait, the deeper the wound.* Mostly, he looked down. Occasionally, he would look up at my desk. Once in the office, he never made eye contact. I sat in my chair, looking as empathetically as I could and I waited and waited. His eyes cased the room. At times, he crossed his arms across his chest, leaned back and looked at the ceiling. Time passed slowly. It was a weighty silence. Ten minutes passed and then twenty minutes. I had lived through other counseling sessions like that, but it didn't make it any easier. Sessions of this nature are exhausting for the therapist as well as the patient. You feel the pain of your client, a sharp, piercing pain.

Time kept ticking away. Thirty minutes … forty minutes. After forty minutes, his body became straight and stiff. His face contorted with intense emotions and tears squeezed out his eyes. He stood up and frantically reached for the Kleenex box. Tears and sobbing soon followed. I waited expectantly for what he would reveal.

"I think I am a homosexual, he said abruptly.

At that moment, nothing would have surprised me. "What makes you think so?" I asked and the floodgates opened.

"When I was ten, I went to boy scout camp in northern Michigan. It was my first time leaving home and going to camp. I shared a small tent with Daryl who was two years older than I was. We had a good time together. We explored the woods, built the most awesome fire, and worked on badges together. At night, we unrolled our sleeping bags and talked until someone yelled, "lights out." We snuggled in between our sleeping bag covers and quieted down. Then it happened."

Ian fell silent again. I was prepared to wait through for another long pause when his emotions suddenly changed. This time there were no tears, only anger.

"I told him to stop, but he didn't. He pushed me into

doing something that I didn't want to do. I felt trapped. I didn't want to yell out. That would have drawn attention to my shame. I just zoned out until it was over. When he was done, he turned over and went to sleep, but I couldn't. I tried to sort it out so I played it over and over again in my mind. All through that miserable night, my mind was racing. The next morning we both acted like nothing happened."

"Was this your first sexual experience?" I asked.

"Yes," he said contritely. After a brief delay, I acknowledged his pain and said,

"Just because your first sexual experience was with a boy, doesn't mean you are a homosexual. You still have all your choices." *He feels so trapped*, I thought. *That trapped feeling can generalize into sexual development. It is so common just to become stuck, not knowing how to get out of that unhappy place.*

I reminded him again that he had all of his choices. "By getting it out in the open and sharing the abuse with someone else, it is no longer a stronghold festering inside of you. Your pain is easing away because it doesn't have a grip on you anymore."

His shoulders relaxed and his breathing pattern changed. After a moment of reflection, he said, "So this horrible experience didn't determine my life or my future? "

"No, not at all. " I noted almost an astonishment in his voice. "Do you find boys, or girls, attractive?"

"What do you mean by attractive.?" he said

"Well, do you find girls or boys particularly charming or alluring? He thought for a moment and said,

"In my English class, Sandy sits next to me and I like her blonde hair and her smile. I look forward to that class so I can see her, but I push it out of my mind because I feel like

I've been ruined. I feel like there is something wrong with me."

"There is *nothing* wrong with you!" I insisted. "Your determination to talk to someone about your inner concerns is truly courageous! Your ability to reflect on the pain and to do something about it is a quality that will help you throughout your life."

We had a few more sessions and Ian was relieved to discover that he was not homosexual. The anger he felt from the sexual abuse, however, was part of the treatment plan and processing that took more time. Interestingly, when we addressed his inner conflict he did much better in his English class. Without this burden, his focus improved, as did his grades. Ian was resilient because he was painfully reflective about himself and sought the help he needed to find an answer to his dilemma. Mental and spiritual agony is created by attributing the wrong causes for outcomes or events. Having the capacity to be reflective, sometimes painfully so, helps us move forward and away from devastatingly wrong turns. The power of reflection is one of the most salient qualities in the transilient individual.

Charles Wesley

Music can be the merciful outcome of painful reflection. One Sunday, bored with the sermon, I read the history of hymns in the back of the hymnal. I was impressed by the endless wellspring of these songwriters. When they reflected on their miserable life, and then, through an epiphany, were unalterably changed, the joy was spectacular. Receiving the extravagant love of God, is so profound and transforming. This awakening has been known to launch timeless musical compositions. One such songwriter, Charles Wesley had a remarkable life story. He muddled through lonely and painful self-reflection to find and feel the love of God. This joy generated over six thousand hymns.

John and Charles Wesley lived their lives in the 1700s, and both were trained at Westminster School and Christ Church in Oxford. John, the older brother was credited with birthing the Methodist movement. In 1727, Charles formed a prayer group with fellow students, but when John, his older brother joined the group, he usurped the leadership role. This defined the direction of the group. Methodical and unusually detailed in their Bible studies they cultivated a disciplined lifestyle. Other students started calling them names, like the "Holy Group," "Sacramentarians," and "Methodists." They had communion every week, fasted regularly, abstained from most forms of entertainment, and frequently visited the sick, the poor, and those in prison. [1]

Charles, bound by stultifying church rules and restrictive legalisms, through a painful and powerful ability to be reflective, became a transformed man. He followed all the rules that were set forth in the group, but his life was joyless. He was empty, and his life meaningless. Out of this painful reflection, he became a changed man. His conversion happened on May 21, 1738 and, from that point in time, he wrote many joyful hymns celebrating his new spiritual freedom.

To know what you don't know is the first step toward understanding. This ability to be reflective shapes us, because it is a vital part of growth-promoting changes. Out of this reflection, we find happier words to describe who we are. Resilient individuals let the pain motivate them to change, which in turn, alters the words they use to describe themselves. When pain motivates, they become seekers to find people who will help them discern truth from untruth. Once the truth is determined, the first step is to become proactive to change the words of your life. Following this reflective process, both Charles and Ian became joyful people. They had this transilient quality in common.

---

[1]

Charles' story begins at his birth. The eighteenth child of Susanna and Samuel Wesley, he was born prematurely just before Christmas, in 1707. As the family story goes, his mother kept him bound in wool blankets until the date he was to be born. When that day came, Charles suddenly opened his eyes on cue and let out a birthing cry as if he somehow knew that was to be his birthday.[2]

There are some parallels there with his early spiritual journey. Before his conversion, he lived a life of pain. He was bound by legalisms and restrictive "holy" routines. The pain of being alienated from his feelings motivated him to seek and find true joy. He felt like he didn't belong. He felt alienated from Christ. In his diary on May 13, 1738 he wrote, "I awoke without Christ, yet still desirous of finding him."[3]

Fortunately, when he experienced his conversion, his spirit awoke and he became free. Ten days later, after his conversion, he wrote, "I felt my heart strangely warmed." Out of his soul came a magnificent flow of freedom that he expressed in music. No longer, were his religious rituals structured and unemotional, they were spontaneous and passionate. Charles vividly testified to his being set free by composing joyous, heartfelt songs, written after his conversion. The first spirit-filled hymn he wrote was *And Can It Be That I Should Gain?* The fourth verse eloquently communicates his release from pain:

Long my imprisoned spirit lay,
Fast bound in sin and nature's night;

2

3

65

Thine eye diffused a quickening ray—
I woke, the dungeon flamed with light;
My chains fell off, my heart was free,
I rose, went forth, and followed Thee.

Some of the familiar songs he composed are: *Hark! The Herald Angels Sing, O for a Thousand Tongues to Sing, Christ the Lord Is Risen Today, Jesus, Lover of My Soul, Rejoice, the Lord is King, Love Divine, All Loves Excelling.*

Throughout his life, he gave passionate sermons out in the fields, and was known as an "Open Air" Preacher. After conversion he stopped drinking, and he remarked,

"I was amazed to find my old enemy, intemperance, so suddenly subdued, that I almost forgot I was ever in bondage to him." His biographer Arnold Dallimore has this to say about his poetry.

"He had inherited the gift from his father, and although it had undoubtedly been resident in him since childhood, his conversion unlocked it and set it free. During his early ministry, he says little in his journal about composing hymns and indeed, this is true throughout his life. But he had within him a treasury of poetry. He constantly experienced the emotions of a true poet, his mind instinctively invested words with harmony and hymn after hymn flowed from his pen."

Charles did have a full life. He was known as a passionate, able preacher, but he also married and had children. He married Sally (Sarah) Gwynne, the daughter of a wealthy magistrate. Although he was primarily focused on his preaching, a journal entry on Thursday, March 24, 1744 he described a perilous journey to meet her parents, [4]

"I resolved to push for Garth finding my strength would never hold out for three more days riding. At five am, I set out in hard rain, which continued all day. We went through perils of water. I was quite gone when we came at night to a little village. There was no fire in the poor hut. A brother supplied us with some wood, nailed up our window and helped us to bed. I had no more rest than the night before."

When he met Sally's parents, they were concerned because Charles had no regular income. So, he quickly and furiously published his book, *Hymns and Sacred Poems*. They were satisfied and the family was later converted to Methodism. Sally and Charles had a good life together. They had seven children, but only three of them survived infancy.

Charles' last hymn was dictated to his wife Sally as he lay on his death bed. It was short and simple but truly profound:

In age and feebleness extreme
Who shall a helpless worm redeem?
Jesus, my only hope Thou art,
Strength of my failing flesh and heart,
Oh, I could catch a smile from Thee
And drop into eternity!

---

[4]

Kathryn Den Houter Ph.D.

Study Questions
The Power of Reflection

1. What do Ian and Charles Wesley have in common? Describe in your own words this transilient quality.

2. How did this transilient quality help them overcome their difficulties?

3. How did this quality help them be resilient (strong, durable?)

4. Do you consider yourself a reflective person? If so, explain a time when being reflective has been helpful. Have you experienced painful reflection? If so, describe that experience. If you do not consider yourself reflective, list three behaviors that you can try that will help you gain this quality.

Chapter Seven
What's My Mission?

I looked at my schedule for the day and noticed that Rachel was my first client. I began speculating. *I wonder what has come up? She was in such a good place when she left counseling. I believe that was only about six months ago. She was three months pregnant and everything seemed to be progressing well.*

I found her file and quickly reviewed the Closed Case Summary. Nothing jumped out at me, so I was mystified. The light on my phone flashed red, letting me know my client was in the waiting room. I stepped out of my office, walked down the short hallway, and opened the waiting room door. Rachel collapsed in my arms. Deep, guttural sobs were all I heard. We hung onto each other for a long time.

"Let's go into my office," I said and guided her to an overstuffed chair so she could relax. "What's going on?" I asked as she slumped into the cushions and sat silent for a long time. She was exhausted and after some time, she started to speak slowly and with much effort.

"I had a baby girl three days ago. She was a beautiful baby. The doctor decided to exchange her blood to treat jaundice." Rachel fell silent again and began to sob. Haltingly she started speaking again. "Air got into the intravenous lines and my sweet Victoria couldn't get the

69

oxygen she needed and she almost died." Rachel heaved a cry and then, fell silent. After a long pause she said, "I handed him a perfect baby and, when she came back, she had black feet."

"Will she recover?" I said horrified.

"I don't know. She was without oxygen so long that they don't know the extent of the damage. There probably will be some brain damage."

Once again, Rachel fell silent and darkness enveloped both of us. We sat motionless, frozen with despair. Deep sadness grabbed our throats and we just couldn't find words.

Rachel was no stranger to tragedy. Her first child Lynn was born with cerebral palsy. She was expecting twins, but one of them died in utero which made her pregnancy high risk. The twin that survived was born with multiple physical handicaps. Lynn's disabilities demanded around the clock care that was exhausting for both Rachel and her husband, Jeff. That 24/7 care continued to the present.

Initially confined to bed, now Lynn had a custom wheel chair that increased her mobility. Daisy, their second daughter is a healthy, vivacious child that has deep empathy for her sisters. Daisy has adapted to her loving, atypical family, and is a delightful child. Jeff and Rachel have a deep spiritual quality about them. This spirituality is the result of enduring a very dark grieving period. Each time they saw their oldest and their youngest daughters, they experienced a painful loss. Two years of work in therapy, and the awakening of their mission created transilient individuals.

The magnitude of their grief would be incomprehensible to many of us. The choices that Rachel and Jeff have made following their initial despair have been exemplary. Following a significant legal settlement with the hospital, Jeff quit his job so he could help Rachel take care of their daughters. Grief counseling helped them manage their anger, to redefine themselves, and to find their mission.

Jeff's journey in therapy was a deeply spiritual one. He reconnected with nature because that was the source of his inner joy. He took camping trips that entailed hiking trails, climbing mountains, and admiring the stars in the sky at night. By pushing his physical limits, he found an inner strength. Once he found his mission, the creation of a family unit filled with healing and joy, he secured a sustainable peace. Finding a powerful mission was his transilient quality.

One late spring day, he pushed both his daughters' wheelchairs through the beautiful forests of northern Michigan. He took delight in pointing out the thimbleberries, the pinecones on the ground, the floating seeds, and the divergent tree barks. This was his form of prayer, a celebration of life. It was crazy and wonderful at the same time.

"I walk by faith, not by sight, " were the first words out of Rachel's mouth in one of our last sessions. "I heard my father say that often and those words keep me going through the dark times."

Rachel expressed herself through poetry. Frequently, she would start a session with a poem she had written during the previous week. They were beautiful words, a written form of prayer. Her poems had the intensity and emotional clarity of Mary Oliver's poetry. They were healing words and she was able to transcend the melancholy of losses through those well-placed words.

Tending to the physical needs of her daughters was exhausting and burdensome. Being alert around the clock was overwhelming, but sometimes there were breathing emergencies with their oldest daughter; Lynn and she didn't trust the hospital or the in-home health care to be as diligent as she was. Her daughters were her mission. Writing was her passion, and her channel to sanity. She was adamant that this misfortune was not going to define her. She wanted a mission that was larger than that.

Both Rachel and Jeff were writers. Jeff had a blog and a newspaper column that demystified the parental role of a child with disability. Rachel wrote poetry that sensitized her audience to and clarified the emotional life of a parent with disabled children. Their collaboration propelled a tremendously insightful mission helping many to better understand the dynamics of disabilities within the context of a family. Their mission is just beginning and the future only knows the extent of the gifts they will give the world. Finding one's mission is a powerful transilient quality. Viktor Frankl, in *Man Searches for Meaning,* aptly clarifies the strength of finding meaning by serving and loving others. [1] "The more one forgets himself—by giving himself to a cause to serve or another person to love—the more human he is and the more he actualizes himself. What is called self-actualization is not an attainable aim at all, for the simple reason that the more one would strive for it, the more he would miss it. In other words, self-actualization is possible only as a side-effect of self-transcendence."

---

[1]

Mother Teresa

Mother Teresa, as of September 4, 2016, has been canonized as a Saint. She never gave birth to her own child but she had millions of children. She saw children ravaged by war, by disease, by disfigurement, by emotional alienation. Was she angry with God for the hurt on their faces? No, this actually motivated her to become more loving, more focused on her children of "pure light." She found the people who were close to death and those that were besieged by disease and poverty were the pure of heart and open to seeing God's face. They felt gratitude when they were anointed with His mercy and the love of Jesus Christ.

Her vision and her mission was to turn their souls to Christ, so they, too, could sing his praises and extol his grace. She was Christ's instrument and referred to herself as "the little bride of Christ." At one point, Saint Teresa said, "By blood, I am Albanian, by citizenship, Indian. By faith, I am a Catholic nun. As to my calling, I belong to the world. As to my heart, I belong entirely to the Heart of Jesus."[2]

She was born in Skopje, Macedonia on August 26, 1910. The next day after her birth, she was baptized as Agnes Gonxha Bojaxhiu. Being born into a devout Catholic family, she learned from a very young age to share what she had and to feed the hungry. Drana Bojaxhiu, her mother, had a deep commitment to charity. She once told her daughter,

"My child, never eat a single mouthful unless you are sharing it with others." Quite often, their household fed the sick and the homeless since visitors who were less fortunate frequented their dinner table. Saint Teresa gave her mother credit for her generosity.

Drana Bojaxhiu was widowed when her daughter was eight years old. This is one of those high impact tragedies that change lives forever. A mystery surrounded her husband's death because he became ill quite suddenly and died. Because of his political views and leadership, he had political enemies and suspicions of poisoning existed.

After the loss of her father, Agnes became even closer to her mother. At age twelve, while on a school pilgrimage to the church of the Black Madonna at Letnice, Kosovo, she received a call to religious life. Her journey took her on a circuitous route, first to Dublin, Ireland. Six years later, after her call at Letnice, she crossed the European continent and sailed to Ireland to join the Sisters of Loreto. She claimed the name Sister Mary Teresa as her own after Saint Therese of Lisieux, who she admired. Taking on a new name was

---

2

symbolic of entering a new phase in her spiritual life. Saint Therese was also known as "the little flower" and was given the title of "the sacred keeper of the garden" by Pope Paul XI.

Once that decision was made, she never saw her mother again. She was committed to being the "little bride of Christ." She spent a year in Dublin and then, For the next part of her journey she was sent to Calcutta, India for her novitiate training period. In May of 1931, made her Profession of Vows.

There she taught at Saint Mary's High School for Girls, which was run by the Loreto Sisters. She learned to speak Bengali and Hindi and her mission was to alleviate poverty through education. Six years later, she took her Final Vows to a life of poverty, chastity, and obedience. It was at that time she added the title of Mother to her name, and from that time on she was known as Mother Teresa until she became a Saint.

She was the principal of the school by 1944 and, through her kindness and generosity, she was an honored member of the faculty, wanting always to be the "light of their lives." After teaching at St. Mary's school for girls in India for seventeen years, she received a "call within a call." This took her life in a new direction.[3]

On September 10, 1946, on a train ride from Calcutta to the Himalayan foothills for a retreat, Christ spoke to her again. He told her to abandon teaching and care for the poorest and sickest in the slums of Calcutta. Since she had taken the oath of obedience, she could not venture out on her

---

[3]

own without permission. She had to lobby the authorities, which she did for a year and a half. Finally, in 1948, they approved her request and she developed a new order called The Sisters of Charity.

She donned a blue and white sari, which became the trademark of her order and she wore this every day for the rest of her life. She obtained six months of medical training and headed out to the streets of Calcutta with a vision of loving and caring for the unwanted. Her order established a hospice for the dying, new centers for the blind, aged, and disabled, as well as a leper colony. This venture had an enormous worldwide impact. She received the Nobel Peace Prize for her humanitarian work. The Sisters of Charity continue to carry on her work around the globe. Mother Teresa was awarded the Jewel of India, the highest honor given to an Indian civilian. The Soviet Union bestowed on her the Gold Medal of the Soviet Peace Committee

She was filled with light and love toward those she helped. Her delightful sense of humor was playful especially with the children she cherished. At times, she doubled over with laughter and people remarked on the glow of her happiness. After her death, however, those close to her were surprised to discover that she suffered for fifty years with what St. John of the Cross described as the "dark night of the soul." She felt alone and abandoned by God.[4] Some describe this experience as a soldier who leaves their beloved behind to go to war. The warrior is confident that his lover will be faithful, so he continues doing what he must without any contact with the one he loves.

4

This describes Mother Teresa. She faithfully and slavishly served Jesus Christ as she tended to the needs of those suffering and dying. She reported a brief period in 1958 when Jesus touched her heart and she felt his presence. This light came during a Mass celebrated shortly after the death of Pope Pius XII, the person who gave her permission to leave the Loreto sisters to work among the poor. "Today my soul is filled with love, with joy untold with an unbroken union of love." Just four weeks later, however, she described the pain of abandonment again to her spiritual director. "He is gone again, leaving me alone." She lived in this darkness until the end of her life, her secret life a living hell.

Mother Teresa died in September, 1997 and beatified in 2003. In December of 2015, Pope Francis recognized a second miracle performed by Mother Teresa, which cleared the way for canonization as a saint. This second miracle was the healing of a man in Santos, Brazil. He had lapsed into a coma from a viral brain infection. His family prayed to Mother Teresa, and he was cured of his symptoms.

Mother Teresa died in September, 1997 and was beatified in 2003. Her transilience came from her enduring mission. So focused, so intent on serving others that she rose above her torment to impart love and warmhearted caring. She infused the world with truth and light.

She truly was a saint.

Study Questions
What's My Mission?

These questions have been carefully crafted to help you get to your transilient self. Answer them the best you can if you are working alone. If you have the support of a group, so much the better, since these questions are designed for group discussion.

1. What do Rachel and Saint Teresa have in common? Describe in your own words this transilient quality.

2. How did this transilient quality help them overcome their difficulties?

3. How did this quality help them be resilient (strong, durable)?

4. Do you have a mission for your life? If so, write it down and share that vision with other members of the group (if you are working in group.) If not determine your values, and from your values determine your mission.

Part Two

The Tools

Kathryn Den Houter Ph.D.

Chapter Eight
S.A.D. J. I. M. L. O. P. E:
Cognitive Behavioral Therapy (CBT)
Stop swimming in mental bacteria

One of the tools I used in my practice that is worth its weight in gold is Cognitive Behavioral Therapy. CBT assumes that, when our thoughts are distorted or unrealistic, we generate psychic pain manifested as anxiety or depression. This can be alleviated when your self-talk changes.

From my twenty-five years as a therapist, I found that the happiest people are the ones who are reality-based in their thinking. According to Judith Beck, Director of the Beck Institute for Cognitive Therapy and Research,[1] cognitive therapy has been based on the research collected from 300 patients. The subjects in the study receive training on how to identify thought distortions, how to modify beliefs, and how to relate to others in different ways. Ultimately, daily behaviors change because their self-talk has changed. Their minds have been renewed by healthy self-talk based on reality.

It takes practice, but once the "pump has been primed" or, to put in another way, once the mind has been stimulated to support successful self-talk, negative moods all but

---

[1]

disappear. Once the positive, rephrased self-statements have been learned and practiced, thinking differently becomes as natural as breathing.

Personally, I found this method helpful when dealing with my own depression. At this time in my life, I'm unlikely to become depressed, because my depressive thoughts instantly shift to reality-based thinking. How we perceive experiences influences how we feel emotionally. Two people often perceive the same situation very differently. One can say, "That's wonderful. I've been waiting for my fortune to change for a long time," whereas the other person might only see the negative, "I always mismanage money and I'll probably do the same with this windfall." Without question, your inner self-talk, either positively or negatively, affects your moods. This impacts your attitudes about living and, ultimately, it affects your physical well-being. With practice, cognitive behavioral therapy can dramatically change your life.

Being realistic can be difficult, especially when we've had a toxic upbringing and our internal talk is undermining and harmful. CBT helps us determine how and when our thoughts are distorted and what thoughts would be healthy replacements. When Annie fell off her bike, the pieces of gravel and sand were imbedded under her skin and she bled profusely. She didn't clean the wound right away and didn't get medical attention. Finally, after several days, she succumbed to a high fever and was forced to see a doctor. The doctor was horrified when he saw Annie, because her wound was swimming in bacteria and fully infected. The doctor scolded her for not taking care of herself.

"Annie, you have to clean a wound right away to stay healthy. Otherwise an infection sets in and your very life is at risk." It is much the same with negative thinking. Our brain is swimming with toxic self-talk, oozing with verbal bacteria and we continue becoming sicker and sicker. We need to tend these "wounds" right away because to ignore them creates emotional emergencies and, in some cases, this depression can be life threatening. Ridding ourselves of this toxic self-talk helps us find our mental health. This undertaking is an ongoing process and we need to cleanse the emotional wounds given by family of origin, teachers, and peers. The dirt and the bacteria of negative self-talk have to be tackled by daily cleanings. It is a matter of hygiene, just like keeping our bodies clean by washing our hands and showering. This helps to insure our physical health. Healthy self-talk needs to be a daily hygiene regimen.

The first step in this routine is checking for levels of anxiety and depression. In the Appendix of this study guide, there are checklists for anxiety and depression. This should be completed once a week. It is a good way to track your progress and to motivate you toward health. Remember, the happiest people are those who are reality-based in their thinking. That is what you want to achieve. Here are some examples of toxic self-talk that need to be changed. These thought distortions are organized by the acronym: S.A.D. J.I.M. L.O.P.E. This is in line with the work done by Judith Beck.[2]

Shoulds: Should statements stop us is our tracks because we feel overwhelmed by all the things we "should" do! Some examples of this are "I should be a kinder person," "I should lose weight," or "I should be more organized."

2

Procrastination happens when two thought distortions—the shoulds and all or nothing thinking—are combined. This kind of thinking tyrannizes us and overwhelms our daily life because our "to do" list is too long. These thoughts make us feel miserable.

All or Nothing statements: These self-statements create pain, because they continually remind us that we're not okay because we're not perfect. Nobody is perfect. All we can do is our best. Here are some distorted self-statements: "I must have perfect attendance at work or I have little to no value for the company." "If I don't get straight As in school, I'm a worthless student," "My family life is not good because we argue," "I'm a good Christian only when I have no impure thoughts and actions," or "I must be perfect or I have no value."

Discounting the positives: This self-talk minimizes positive comments that people make and give us feelings of inferiority: "When people say I'm a good mother, I know they are just trying to be nice, they don't really mean it," "If my classmates say that I'm a good writer, they are being sarcastic," "When my mom tells me that I'm lovable, she has to say it because she's my mother," "I discount complements from my husband, because he has ulterior motives," or "He says I look nice only because he wants me to feel better."

Jumping to judgments: This is a very common distortion and, if not changed, it can lead to difficult relationships. Here are some examples: "She looked at me funny, so I don't think she likes me," "He didn't answer me because he thought my comment was stupid," "They didn't come to my birthday party because they don't like me," "I never get any visitors because I have an ugly house," or "I would prepare for the test more, but no matter what I do, I always do poorly."

Inappropriate use of definitives: This distortion uses *always* and *never*: "I am sad and unhappy all day, every day," "My mother always puts me down," "He never gives me a break," "Nobody ever appreciates me," or "Everybody I see thinks that I don't have any abilities."

Misplaced negatives: This self-talk happens when someone sees only the negative side to life, (which is only part of reality). These are some of those self-statements: "I will never amount to much," "My teachers have it out for me," "My husband and other relatives use me," "Happiness always eludes me," or "I will die before I decide what I want to do."

Labeling incorrectly: This thought distortion puts the wrong label on yourself or others. This creates a skewed sense of reality. The healthiest approach is to label yourself accurately so that your thoughts stay reality-based. Some of these negative self-statements are: "I am always a moody person," "I'm always a loser," "My boyfriend says I am flaky so I'm a flaky person," "I'm stupid," "I'm always fearful," or "I'm unhappy so I'm a depressed person. "

Overgeneralization: When you see only negative outcomes, it leads to patterns of defeat and misery. "I woke up this morning, stubbed my toe, so the rest of the day will be miserable," "My co-worker looked at me funny this morning, so I will have a bad workday," or "I flunked my first math test, so I will flunk all the rest of them and flunk out of my math class."

Personalizing to the extremes: This self-talk manifests when one attributes bad occurrences to the wrong person. "If I only would have been a better parent, then my son would have excelled in school," "All my daughter's problems started when I didn't help her do her homework," or "My divorce is my fault because I didn't go to college."

Emotional thoughts inappropriately placed: Our feelings change so often, it becomes a distortion when you attribute your feelings to a longstanding problem. "I feel stupid, therefore, I *am* stupid," "I feel fat, so I *am* fat," or "I feel like a loser, so I *am* a loser."

The Power of the REPHRASE:

This next step, the mechanics of changing the bacteria laden self-talk to reality based self-talk, will probably be the most important one you'll take in your life. First of all, circle the thought distortions that apply to you and then on a separate sheet of paper write down self-statements that you say to yourself.

If you listen closely to what you're saying to yourself, you will hear these distortions over and over again. Sound the alarm! Raise the flags! These internal negative thoughts *must* change. It is critical for good mental health.

I'll rephrase the examples that I gave for each thought distortion. First up is the "shoulds" then the "all or nothing" statements. The next distortion rephrased is "discounting the positives" followed by "jumping to judgments." Then, "inappropriate use of always and never" and "more negatives than what is real," and "labeling one's self incorrectly." The last three are "overgeneralizations," "personalizing to the extreme" and, finally, "emotional thoughts inappropriately placed." All of these contribute to the acronym: S. A. D. J. I. M. L. O. P. E.

The key here is to find the distortions that are true for you, and then rephrase them so they are healthy. Once this rephrasing is done, practice them faithfully so they become automatic. To your amazement, your symptoms of anxiety and depression will decrease or disappear. (See appendix for blank practice diagrams)

Example 1

Name_____ Date_____

Thought Distortion:

Shoulds:	Current Self-Statements	Healthy Rephrase
	I should be a kinder person.	I will find two ways of being kinder.
	I should lose weight.	I will set reasonable weight goals.
	I should be more Organized.	I will choose an area to organize.

Helpful hint: "I should" is changed to "I will" and then, what follows the 'I will' is very "doable" and *not* overwhelming.

Example 2

Name_____ Date_____

Thought Distortion:

All or Nothing Statements	Current Self-Statements	Healthy Rephrase
	I must have perfect attendance or I have no value at work.	There are more ways to determine value.
	If I don't get straight, "A's" in school, I'm	Getting all "A's" is not the only quality of a good student.

	worthless.	
	My family life is not good because we argue.	Arguing can be good sometimes.
	I am a good Christian only when I have no impure thoughts.	I might not be a perfect Christian, but I'm good enough.
	I must be perfect, or I have no value.	All I have to be is good enough.

Helpful hint: Remember that all we have to be is "good enough" since perfection is not possible. Remind yourself of that!

Example 3

Name_____ Date_____

Thought Distortion:

Discounting the Positives:	Current Self-statements	Healthy Rephrase
	When people say I am a good mother, I know they just trying to be nice, they don't really mean it.	They wouldn't take the time to say it if they didn't mean it.
	If my classmates say that I am a good writer, they are being sarcastic.	I will allow the positive comment to make me feel good inside.

	When my mom says that I am lovable, she has to say it because she is my mom.	I will let her love come inside and let it make me feel good.
	I discount compliments from my husband because he has ulterior motives.	I can't read his mind, so I will let it soak in.
	He says I look nice because he wants me to feel better.	Feeling better is a good thing – Don't knock it.

Helpful hint: When we push positives comments away, we are choosing to live in misery. We have a choice here.

Example 4

Name_____ Date_____

Thought Distortion:

Jumping to judgments:	Current Self-statements	Healthy Rephrase
	She looked at me funny so I don't think she likes me.	I am not a mind reader. I don't have all the information.
	He didn't look at me because he thought my answer was stupid.	Get all the facts before you determine what is going on.
	They didn't come to my birthday party	There are many other reasons they

	because they don't like me.	didn't come.
	I never get any visitors because I have an ugly house.	Get all the facts before you jump to a conclusion.
	I would prepare for the test but no matter what I do, I always do poorly.	I will do a better analysis of why I do poorly on tests.

Helpful hint: Remember that you are not a mind reader, and that it is important to get all the information before you come to a conclusion. Otherwise, you will feel badly unnecessarily.

Example 5

Name_____ Date_____

Thought Distortion:

Inappropriate use of always and never:	Current Self-statements	Healthy Rephrase
	I am always sad every day.	In all honesty, my feelings change every day.
	He never gives me a break.	Some days are better than others.
	Nobody ever appreciates me.	I will learn to appreciate myself.
	Everybody I meet thinks I don't	I can't read minds and how I feel about

	have any ability.	myself is what is important.

Helpful hint: Remember to be accurate when appraising yourself. To overestimate or underestimate yourself will present problems for you, so be honest.

Example 6

Name_____ Date_____

Thought Distortion:

More negative than what is real:	Current Self-statements	Healthy Rephrase
	My teachers have it out for me.	I will get the big picture and not focus on the negatives.
	My husband and my other relatives use me.	I will stand back and decide when they are using me and when they are not and will act accordingly. I will point out the use.
	I will die before I decide what I want to do.	It is hard but not impossible to make decisions. I have made good decisions before.

Helpful hint: Once again, be clear about reality. It is not all bad. Think about the good part of reality as well.

Example 7

Name_____ Date_____

Thought Distortion:

Labeling one's self incorrecty:	Current Self-Statements	Healthy Rephrase
	I am always a moody person.	To be truthful, there are more days when I am not moody.
	I am a loser.	Sometimes I win and sometimes I lose.
	My boyfriend says I am flaky so I am flaky.	I will think for myself, and in my opinion there are times when I am reliable.
	I am stupid.	In reality, I am smart in many areas.
	I am always fearful.	In many situations, I have conquered my fears.
	I am unhappy so I am a depressed person.	Being sad doesn't always make me a depressed person.

Helpful hint: Be ACCURATE when you talk to yourself about yourself. It makes a huge difference.

Example 8

Name_____ Date_____

Thought Distortion:

Overgeneralizations:	Current Self-statements	Healthy Rephrase
	I woke up this morning, stubbed my toe, so the rest of the day will be miserable.	Just because the day started that way doesn't mean that it will end that way.
	My co-worker looked at me funny this morning so I will have a bad day.	One funny look does not equal a bad day.
	I flunked my first math test so I will flunk all the rest of them.	There are many things I can do to keep that from happening. Many options are open.

Helpful hint: It is important not to heap misery on top of misery. Stop and intervene so the outcomes are favorable.

Example 9

Name_____ Date_____

Thought Distortion:

Personalizing to Extremes:	Current Self-statements	Healthy Rephrase
	If only I had been a better person, my son would have excelled in school.	My son is his own person and he needs to be responsible for how he does in school.
	All my daughter's problems started when I didn't help her do her homework.	My daughter needs to take responsibility for her own homework.
	My divorce is my fault because I didn't go to college.	It takes two people to create problems in marriage.

Helpful hint: Blaming yourself is not helpful. If you are responsible for some of the problems, accept that and learn from it. Taking the entire blame is NOT helpful to you or anyone else. It is a distortion of reality.

Example 10

Name_____ Date_____

Thought Distortion:

Emotional thoughts inappropriately placed:	Current Self-statements	Healthy Rephrase
	I feel stupid, therefore I am stupid.	My feelings change all the time and they are not factual.
	I feel fat, so I am fat.	Feelings do not determine the facts of the situation.
	I feel like a loser, so I am a loser.	Just because you feel like a loser does not make you a loser. Feelings are changeable.

Helpful hint: Feelings are not reliable indicators of what reality is. Remember the happiest people are those that are reality-based in their thinking.

Study Questions
Cognitive Behavioral Therapy

These questions have been carefully crafted to help you get to your transilient self. Answer them the best you can if you are working alone. If you have the support of a group, so much the better, since these questions are designed for group discussion.

1. If you haven't done so, identify your distortions. Turn your negative self-talk into healthy talk. Look at the examples that are in Chapter 9.

2. Do the Anxiety Checklist and the Depression Checklist (found in Appendix) before you rephrase the negative thoughts and then, after you have practiced rephrasing for a week. Note the difference. Do you see a difference? Describe the difference.

3. Practice these rephrases until they are automatic. Indicate whether you have seen an improvement in your anxiety and/or depression.

4. Have others in your immediate family or friends seen a difference in you?

Chapter Nine
From Stress to Relaxation: Three Steps

1. Step One: Become aware of what stress does to your body. Understand how stress affects you.

2. Step Two: Prevent stress in your life by changing perspectives, setting goals and improving relationships.

3. Step Three: Cancel the ill effects of stress. This is done through relaxation, visualization exercising and good sleeping habits.

Step One: Understanding how stress affects you.

Some clients have found themselves in treatment because of overwhelming stress. They find themselves spinning out of control and immobilized by fear. Sensing they were ready to listen to a therapist, I discuss in great detail what stress does to harm our minds and bodies.

Surprised by the insidious nature of it, they are open to discussing the ill effects of stress. The first step is becoming conscious of how stress can be harmful. From a physical perspective, the two biggest problems are the release of cortisol and pumping adrenalin into the system. The following diagram illustrates this biochemical process.

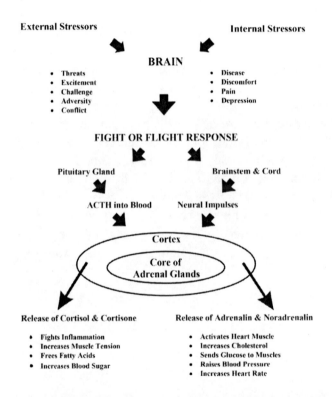

External stressors such as outside threats, challenges, adversity, physical ailments, and conflicts incite a fight or flight response which then prompts the pituitary gland to pump ACTH, the hormone produced by the pituitary gland into the core of the adrenal glands. When this happens, cortisol and cortisone are released, which helps the body deal with stress. It fights inflammation, increases muscle tension, frees fatty acids, and increases blood sugar. However, when stress is longstanding, it is hard on the heart and blood vessels and the circulatory system is jeopardized.

Internal stressors such as disease, discomfort, pain and depression, also activate the fight or flight response. This response is channeled through the brainstem and spinal cord, which incites neural impulses. The neuronal impulses set off the adrenal gland, which releases adrenalin and noradrenalin. These hormones in turn, activate the heart muscle, increase cholesterol, send glucose to the muscles, raises blood pressure, and increase heart rate. Stress in the short term can actually be beneficial, but if it becomes unrelenting and prolonged, it will wreak havoc within the body.

The adrenal glands are on the front lines of the battle with stress, but so is the autonomic nervous system. This system is responsible for bodily functions, which are not consciously directed, such as breathing, heartbeat, and digestion. However, through relaxation, training, and visualization, these functions can be impacted and can create healthy stress responses.

The Autonomic Nervous System

ORGAN OR FUNCTION	FIGHT/FLIGHT (sympathetic)	REST/RELAXATION (parasympathetic)
Heart Rate	Increased	Decreased
Arteries		
Peripheral	Constricted	Dilated
Deep	Dilated	-----------
Blood Pressure	Increased	Decreased
Blood Sugar	Increased	Decreased
Respiration Rate	Increased	Decreased
Gastrointestinal Activity	Decreased	Increased
Skin		
Sweat Glands	Increased	Decreased
Hair Follicles	Contract/Erect	Relaxed

Do you get headaches? Neck and back pain? Have you been losing hair or experiencing skin rashes? Do you have stomach upsets due to hassles with heartburn? If the answer is "yes," your body is probably telling you that you are dealing with too much stress, which causes wear and tear on your body.

All of us have body "hot spots" that yell "help" when you have too much stress. For instance, your stomach might generate too much acid; breathing becomes labored. Because there are genetic patterns here, if mom and dad had stomach problems, it's quite likely that you will too. Body "hot spots" are different for everybody, but the message is the same: REDUCE THE STRESS! Please complete this *Stress Symptoms Checklist* to discover where your body accumulates stress.

STRESS SYMPTOMS

Common Symptoms	How Often (circle)			Happens When Stressed (circle)	
Aches/Neck/Shoulders	Rarely	Sometimes	Frequently	Yes	No
Appetite Loss/Increase	Rarely	Sometimes	Frequently	Yes	No
Backache	Rarely	Sometimes	Frequently	Yes	No
Blurry Vision	Rarely	Sometimes	Frequently	Yes	No
Cough	Rarely	Sometimes	Frequently	Yes	No
Cramps	Rarely	Sometimes	Frequently	Yes	No
Diarrhea	Rarely	Sometimes	Frequently	Yes	No
Dizziness	Rarely	Sometimes	Frequently	Yes	No
Dry Mouth	Rarely	Sometimes	Frequently	Yes	No
Excessive Sweating	Rarely	Sometimes	Frequently	Yes	No
Face Hot/Flushed	Rarely	Sometimes	Frequently	Yes	No
Fatigue	Rarely	Sometimes	Frequently	Yes	No
Frequent Urination	Rarely	Sometimes	Frequently	Yes	No
Hands/Feet-Cold/Clam	Rarely	Sometimes	Frequently	Yes	No
Heartburn	Rarely	Sometimes	Frequently	Yes	No
High Blood Pressure	Rarely	Sometimes	Frequently	Yes	No
Hyperventilation	Rarely	Sometimes	Frequently	Yes	No
Impotence	Rarely	Sometimes	Frequently	Yes	No
Insomnia	Rarely	Sometimes	Frequently	Yes	No
Itching/Rashes	Rarely	Sometimes	Frequently	Yes	No
Grinding Teeth	Rarely	Sometimes	Frequently	Yes	No
Late Menstruation	Rarely	Sometimes	Frequently	Yes	No
Loss of Hair	Rarely	Sometimes	Frequently	Yes	No
Muscle Spasms	Rarely	Sometimes	Frequently	Yes	No
Nail Biting	Rarely	Sometimes	Frequently	Yes	No
Palpitations	Rarely	Sometimes	Frequently	Yes	No

Rapid Heart Beat	Rarely	Sometimes	Frequently	Yes	No
Stomach Upsets	Rarely	Sometimes	Frequently	Yes	No
Tapping Feet/Fingers	Rarely	Sometimes	Frequently	Yes	No
Trembling Legs	Rarely	Sometimes	Frequently	Yes	No
Vaginal Discharge	Rarely	Sometimes	Frequently	Yes	No

This inventory is an adaptation of the Patient Health Questionnaire (PHQ-15)

Do you see a pattern? If the words "frequently" and "yes" are circled often, then probably stress is at least partly responsible for the way you are feeling. But even if there is no clear pattern of stress - see your doctor since there might be an underlying medical condition that could be causing your symptoms. What follows this checklist is an **Over the Past Year Inventory.** This can explain some of the stress you are feeling. I would recommend that you complete this one to get a fuller picture of what is going on.

What on Earth is Causing my Stress?

Now you know the body signals of stress. Next, it is critical to know what is causing this stress. This is an adaptation of The Social Readjustment Rating Scale developed by Thomas Holmes and Richard Rahe.[1] Complete this *Over the Past Year Inventory* to learn more:

Life Experiences	How Many	Multiple	Total
Death in Family		10	
Separation/Divorce		12	
Injury/Illness		8	
Married		7	
Fired		7	
Retired		7	
Illness in the Family		7	
Pregnancy/Miscarriage		6	
Sexual Problems		6	
Business Changes		6	
Major financial Struggle		6	
Death of a Close Friend		6	
Job Change		6	
Mortgage Debt		4	
Foreclosure		4	
Empty Nest		4	
Good Friend Left		4	
Troubling In-laws		4	
Won Award/Recognized		4	

---

[1]

Spouse in/out of work		4	
Graduation		4	
Changed Residence		3	
Ceased Smoking/Drink		3	
Diet Changes		2	
Work-related Problems		3	
School Change		3	
Difficulty Sleeping		2	

15-29 – Low stress load in past year
20-49 - Moderate stress load
50 + High stress load

Total _____

Step Two: How to prevent stress.

After the identifying stress and becoming aware of how it affects your body, it is time to find ways to remove stress from your life. Your perspective on life is key to reducing stress. Robert L. Woolfolk, in his book, *Stress, Sanity and Survival,* outlines the very best of this "life-perspective" mindset.[2]

First of all, it is important to remember that it is *not* what happens to us that makes life stressful, but it is what we tell ourselves about these events that creates stressful emotions. Second, it is pivotal that we understand that we can never pursue happiness as the final goal. When we do

---

[2]

this we are self-focused and we keep asking ourselves; "Am I happy now?" or "Why am I not happy now?" These questions lead to self-preoccupation, and self-preoccupied people are rarely happy. Happiness comes when you do something enjoyable and the truth of happiness is becoming other-focused.

Another consideration is the importance of finding activities that give you intrinsic satisfaction. This happens when just doing the activity is fun. The fun disappears when you have to perform to other's expectations. Also, finding a sense of purpose whether it be a dedication to a person, an idea, or set of values, acts as a compass that reduces stress as you travel through life. The chief guideline for a low stress lifestyle is the acceptance of your own shortcomings. When you surrender the notion that you have control over what ultimately happens to you, this acceptance gives you peace of mind.

Be benevolent. Benevolence counteracts hostility and draws people to you. This reduces stress and uncertainty. Learning to tolerate and forgive, both yourself and others, is critical in stress reduction. When you are intolerant of your own frailties, it leads to low self-esteem and this intolerance spills over onto others and leads to blame and anger. Exercise compassion by seeing the world and yourself through the eyes of others. We reduce stress when we understand the viewpoints of others. Empathy, too, is the remedy for blame and anger, so use empathy often as well.

To be a happy person you must take responsibility for your own happiness. No other person can make you feel secure and happy over the long haul. You must do this for yourself. Blaming others for your unhappiness is simply a waste of time. Another important consideration is acknowledging that a low stress lifestyle is a reasonably efficient and well-managed one. Sloppiness and disorganization create more stress than they remove. When taking charge of your life, remember that life's challenges never end and that there will always be new and different challenges to face. Looking for a happy ending to all your troubles is futile, because that day will never come. When you stop waiting for that perfect outcome, then you can relax and savor each moment. Most memorable joys in life are short-lived, enjoy them thoroughly when they come.

The most significant component of a low-stress life is to recover from previous struggles. When you have recovered, shut the book on them and put them behind you. When this is accomplished, you are free to enjoy each new day.

What we know about aging is that stress compounds the process. To retard the inevitable, Deepak Chopra in his book, *Ageless Realities, a Guidebook*[3] suggests developing practices that will promote fulfilling relationships and job satisfaction. Laughing often, expressing feelings, and optimistic thinking all slow down aging. Living within financial means, developing healthy daily routines, and above all, taking responsibility for your own happiness are keys to staying younger.

Chopra has some practical suggestions, too: reduce caffeine and sugar, eat a healthy, nutritious diet, and perform regular aerobic exercise. Cultivate an 80% success rate rather than 100%. This change in standards has a greater success rate and keeps you from "pulling your hair out." Express your feelings with control and label them accurately. Learning to identify which circumstances incite

---

[3]

negative emotions is critical. Find ways to manage those circumstances. Sometimes avoiding those toxic situations is best. Improving your relationships quells much stress in your life. Create networks of supportive contacts and then, establish a level of comfort when asking for help. Communicating feelings with others fosters assertiveness and strong, effective relationships. When you can, delegate tasks and develop conflict-management strategies. Far-reaching and lasting positive effects are generated when you become proactive rather than reactive. Seek information to help you solve problems, set goals to achieve success, and break large tasks into smaller tasks so they become more manageable.

Finally, surround yourself with an environment that exudes calm. Produce an aesthetically pleasing one with personalized pictures and plants. Jettison machines that don't work, and eliminate excess noise. Find a quiet zone in your space that will renew you and, most of all, reduce relationship conflict in your environment.

Step Three: Canceling the ill effects of stress.

Once we are tied-up in knots with stress, what do we do about it? How do we cancel the ill effects of stress? Cold hands signal that you need "on-the-spot" recovery from stress. Because circulation is constricted due to tense muscles, your extremities are cold. Tense neck muscles contribute to lightheadedness because blood cannot move freely to the brain. Here are some quick remedies for tension:

"On-the-Spot" Recovery from Stress

- 1. VISUALIZE A RELAXING SCENE: my favorite scene is imagining myself at a beach under an umbrella. I am slowly slipping my hand beyond the shade of the umbrella into the warm sun. Feel the radiant warmth. Through mental focus, I can actually feel my hands becoming warm. With visualization, I have found these results to be quite amazing.
- 2. MOVE INTO A PROBLEMS-SOLVING MODE: emotional reactivity can be unlearned by using the benefits of deep relaxation training. We can learn how to recover quickly from upsetting experiences by shifting mental gears to, "How can I solve this problem?" The focus shifts from powerlessness to proactivity.
- 3. GIVE YOURSELF SPACE (A THINKING BREAK): Rather than becoming involved in the ill effects of stress say, either to others or yourself, "I can't answer that right now, let me think it over."
- 4. THOUGHT STOPPING: When your mind is filled with troublesome thoughts (I call them junk mail), you need to remove them from your field of consciousness. Clean the slate by telling your mind to *"Stop."* It will listen to you and stop. In the interim, fill your mind with more positive thoughts.
- 5. REHEARSING SUCCESS: This technique helps you shift your thinking from situations that are out of your control to a bigger picture with a successful outcome. Mentally create a "mind movie" with you as the lead character. Repeat the scene in your mind until you feel comfortable with your success. Your anxiety will be reduced as you become more accepting of your success.

Get Yourself Ready to Relax

Create a setting that is just right, so you can gain the most from relaxation. Herbert Benson, in *The Relaxation Response,* outlines four conditions:

- **1. A Quiet Environment**
  Choose a place free from interruptions. Turn your phone off, close the shades, put a DO NOT DISTURB sign on your door. This is *your time* You deserve it and need it!

- **2. A Mental Device**
  Most of the time we need a constant source of internal stimulation, which helps us   switch off outside distractions. This device can be a word or a phrase, a candle, a metronome, a relaxation CD or a fixed object on the wall.

- **3. A Passive Attitude**
  Don't try too hard! Avoid thinking about how you are doing or if you are getting it right. It takes most people three or four weeks of practice to begin to feel like they've got the "hang of it." Each person responds uniquely to relaxation exercises, so don't worry if your experience is different. Distracting thoughts are common so gently bring yourself back to relaxation.

- **4. A Comfortable Position**
  Find a position that is comfortable and that supports your whole body. Some people practice in a comfortable, straight-backed chair, others recline on a bed. Make sure your neck, back and knees are supported when lying down. If you fall asleep, try a different time of the day or change to a sitting position.

Deep Breathing Exercise

When you are at peace with yourself, your breathing is naturally slow, deep, and regular. When you are upset or stressed, your breathing rate speeds up and each breath becomes shallower. By deliberately controlling your breathing you can make it slower and induce a state of calm. You can actually use your breathing to quiet your mind, ease your stress and relax your body. Breathing right is healing. Here are some tips:

- Sit upright in a chair with your arms at your sides and your feet flat on the floor.
- Avoid touching your skin because skin-to-skin contact breaks concentration. Crossed legs and arms can "fall asleep" and become a distraction.
- Focus on the end of your nose. Take a deep breath in, feel the coolness in your nostrils and down your throat. Allow the air to expand your chest and abdomen and push your stomach out.
- As you are breathing in, say, "Just," and, then, as you let go, breathe out and say, "Relax."
- Think of this as a circular process. Never hold your breath at either the top or bottom of the breathing cycle to keep it smooth.
- Keep your attention focused on the feelings you experience by concentrating on the phrase, "Just ... relax."
- The benefits of breathing right include both relaxation and increased levels of energy.
- Practice this exercise for about ten minutes two times a day for the rest of your life.

Kathryn Den Houter Ph.D.

- This form of Yoga breathing can be practiced at all times. Practice while sitting at a traffic light, during a break at work, while exercising/walking, or during meal times.

Autogenic Relaxation

In the past, it was assumed that body functions were beyond our conscious control, but our understanding has changed. Autogenic exercises actually use your conscious thoughts to influence the way your body functions. These exercises use the process of intense concentration and the power of suggestion to produce a state of deep relaxation. There are three stages in Autogenic Relaxation Training:

- **The Mood Stage:** This stage creates a mental atmosphere for the acceptance of suggested change. It is important to use your critical faculties to understand how much better it would be for you if you didn't have the unwanted behavior. With that awareness, your mood becomes one of serene anticipation of success.
- **The Relaxation Stage:** Before you move into the relaxation stage, close your eyes and become aware of your thinking. Recall a recent time when you were worried or afraid of something. Relive the details. Now, ask yourself "Is this how I want to feel?" The answer being "No," *shift* your thoughts to the positive by seeing yourself as courageous and confident. Revel in those thoughts, and with those sublime feelings slip into a mental state that embodies that idyllic place. Once there, while using the most effective method of relaxation, your resolve will be strengthened. You will see yourself as confident, courageous, and having healthy self-control.

- **The Final or Change Stage**
  After this deep relaxation, change the image you have of yourself from a problem sufferer to a problem solver who is becoming more at peace. In the area of self-improvement, Autogenic Training applications are virtually limitless. They can be used to: 1. relieve allergies, 2. lessen cold symptoms, 3. get rid of IBS, 4. improve skin conditions, 5. end pesky headaches. In all cases, the basic procedure is the same: *You* set the mood. *You* relax deeply. *You* mentally make the change.

  Learning to relax is so important, because it cancels out the ill effects of stress. Always remember to be patient with yourself. Relaxation is a skill that is acquired with practice. Trying too hard can be discouraging and the worst that can happen is that you give up. though many people experience some benefits of relaxation after the first session, the most significant benefits of relaxation begin to occur after about six to ten practice sessions.

  Regular daily practice is the key to learning the relaxation response. Try to practice at about the same time each day. Some like to practice in the morning so they have a relaxed start to the day. Others find that relaxation practice helps smooth the transition from work to personal time and some prefer relaxing before bedtime, so they sleep well. I move into relaxation whenever I feel my hands getting cold because this is my signal that I am stressed. Relaxing at this time is so helpful because, when the body is relaxed, the blood circulates to your extremities and they become warm. Sometimes daily occurrences prohibit me from relaxing on the spot, but I make time later to relax as soon as I'm able. "On-the-spot" recovery from stress helps me out in a pinch as well.

113

Also, remember that learning to relax is paradoxical. In order to gain self-control, you must give up control. Letting go is the key. You will feel the negativity evaporate when your thoughts become calm. It is imperative that you allow enough time to complete the relaxation exercise. The time it takes to develop the relaxation response is less than the average sitcom, and the benefits are far greater. Practice regularly, for about six to nine months, and you will be forever changed in a positive way.

Another technique that I have used and tested in my personal life is the Delta Sleeping Technique. Delta waves were discovered in the early 1900s by W. Grey Walter.[4] He found that the Delta waves were associated with the very deepest levels of sleep, relaxation, and peace of mind. The frequency range of the Delta waves is 0-4Hz, which is the slowest of all the brainwaves. When these slow waves constitute our sleep, we wake up feeling refreshed and rejuvenated. Further, it helps the healing process and it stabilizes many unconscious functions of our body like our heartbeat, digestion, breathing to name just a few. In some cases, Delta Waves help slow down the aging process through the production of hormones like DHEA and melatonin. It improves the immune system and keeps everything "in-sync" and in good working order. The following technique uses visualization and autosuggestion to help you get into the Delta frequency, so your night's sleep can be restorative. If you struggle with sleeping, give this technique a try. You will be blessed with a good night's sleep.

4

Healthy Sleeping – The Delta Technique

Healthy sleep means a healthy life. The Delta Technique has proved to be indispensable for me. This approach offers a sure fire way to get to the world of sleep. This is an imaginary technique you can use to enter natural, normal sleep, anytime, anywhere without the use of drugs. When you need to use the Sleep Technique, begin with whatever relaxation technique helps you into a deep state of relaxation.

Mentally visualize a chalkboard. Have chalk in one hand, an eraser in the other. If possible, identify what it is that is keeping you awake and let it be symbolized by a Z. If you cannot specifically identify what's keeping you awake, then let the Z symbolize the unknown.

Mentally draw a large circle on the chalkboard. Write a big Z within the circle. Proceed to erase the Z from within the circle starting at the center, being careful not to erase the circle. You are removing whatever was keeping you from peaceful, calm, restful sleep.

Once you erase the Z from within the circle, to the right and outside the circle, mentally take your chalk and write the word *deeper*. Every time you write the word deeper, you'll enter that deeper, healthier level of relaxation in the direction of natural, peaceful, calm, restful, normal sleep.

Continue with the numbers 98, 97, 96, 95, 94, and so on, on a descending scale until you get to zero. If done correctly, you should be asleep, but if you are still awake return to 98 and count on a descending scale until asleep.

The disrupting thoughts are blocked out by counting the numbers.

Whenever you use the Sleep Technique, you will enter natural, peaceful, calm, restful, normal, healthy sleep, anytime, anywhere, without the use of drugs. Whenever you enter sleep with the use of the Sleep Technique, if someone calls you or in case of danger or in an emergency, you will open your eyes, feeling alert, responsive, calm, and refreshed. You will awaken at your customary, or assigned, time and be wide-awake, feeling fine.

In summary, this chapter has demonstrated: 1. The importance of becoming conscious about what stress is doing to your body and emotions, 2. Ways to prevent stress in your daily life and 3. How to cancel the ill effects of stress through relaxation exercises. Relaxation training was the backbone of my therapeutic approach because it enabled growth. Change is facilitated when a client feels less anxious and more comfortable in their own skin. Relaxation provides the best atmosphere for change.

Study Questions
From Stress to Relaxation

These questions have been carefully crafted to help you get to your transilient self. Answer them the best you can if you are working alone. If you have the support of a group, so much the better, since these questions are designed for group discussion.

Question 1: Are You a Stress Survivor? (Answer "yes" or "no" to the following questions.)

1. Do you have interest in your job? Do you like what you're doing?

2. Do you have the capacity to play?

3. Do you have a balance between your logical and creative self?

4. Are you curious and enjoy exploring new ideas?

5. Can you express your feelings and communicate well with others?

6. Are you able to balance work, love, and play in your life?

7. Are you honest in how you appraise yourself?

8. Can you switch roles? Are you adaptable?

9. Are you able to go with what feels right for you?

10. Do you find an inner-resilience no matter what happens to you?

Question 2: Choose one from the above list with a "no" response and create realistic goals that will help you get closer to being a "stress survivor." Establish three steps to help you implement your goal.

Goal:

Step 1.

Step 2.

Step 3.

Question 3: Have you been able to develop a low stress lifestyle? (Answer "yes" or "no" to the following questions:)

1. Do you monitor what you say to yourself during stressful situations?

2. Have you found activities that you really enjoy doing?

3. Does helping others make you feel happy?

4. Do you have guiding principles that help you during stressful times?

5. Have you been able to accept that you have little control over what will ultimately happen to you?

6. Do you have a good sense of humor that is not hostile or cynical?

7. Are you able to forgive yourself and others?

8. Do you see the world through the eyes of others? Are you empathetic?

9. Have you taken responsibility for your own sense of well-being?

10. Do you have an efficient, well-managed daily life?

11. Have you set aside the fantasy that one day all your problems will be over? Have you learned to savor each day as it comes?

12. Have you worked through and closed the book on past issues making you free to enjoy each day?

Question 4: How will you make your life less stressful? Choose one low stress guideline from the list above and set a goal. Add three steps for your goal.

Chapter Ten
Visualization

Ironically, the human nervous system cannot distinguish the difference between real circumstances and a mental process as long as the mind's eye sees it in vibrant detail. According to Maxwell Malta in his book, *Psycho-Cybernetics*,[1] progress is made by utilizing both strategies: practice through actual experience and practice through visualization of the activity utilizing imagination. Tremendous gains are made by rehearsing successes. There are significant changes in self-image and self-esteem.

Abraham Lincoln espoused visualization as a vital component of determination.[2] "Always bear in mind that your own resolution to succeed is more important than any other one thing," he said. He believed that failure, like success, comes from a place within. For instance, seeing it happen goes a long way to *having* it happen. For example, if you want to be a lawyer, see yourself as a lawyer. By seeing it happen, you were well on your way to making it happen. Lincoln advised a young man who was struggling with school, "I know not how to aid you, save in the assurance of one of mature age, and much severe experience, that you cannot fail if you resolutely determine, that you *will not*."

1

2

One of Abraham Lincoln's lawyer friends, Ward Lamon, clearly remembered his determination to become President. He visualized it, willed it and it materialized. "I will get there," Lincoln would say with clear resolve.

Visualization as a psychotherapeutic technique is indispensable. I used this method liberally with my clients, because visualizing a healthy state of mind is the first step toward getting there. "How do you see yourself when therapy is over?" I would say and, then, the therapeutic work would begin. They would develop a lengthy list of personal goals that would mold them into the person they wanted to be. Usually the list was an exhaustive one. Once created, we spent several sessions developing those goals.

Beginning in the month of August and throughout the fall, I spent much of my time doing visualizations with children of school age. School anxiety would begin as early as the week after the 4th of July, filling children with concern.

"Will I like my teachers? Will they like me? Will my friends be in my class or will I be all alone?" Their concerns would go on and on. As soon as the school made the list of teachers public, they brought in their list. We would discuss their fears and then visualize how to handle those fears using behaviors that produced confidence. Together we decided how the student wanted the school year to turn out and then we visualized our way through to a desirable conclusion.

The best way to understand the process is to give an example:

The first step was determining the outcome. In this case, Joe a seventh grader wanted to get along with his teachers, get good grades, be successful in a sport, find some good friends and feel more confident. Would he get along with his

121

teachers? That was a big part of his concern. Mr. Hiccombs was his social studies teacher and his soccer coach. Ms. Schwester was his English teacher and study hall monitor. Mr. Strommer was his math and science teacher and his basketball coach.

"Well, Joe, what have you heard about Mr. Hiccombs?"

"My sister had him two years ago," he replied, "and he is really tough and hard to please, but my sister said she learned lots of new stuff from him."

"What kind of student does he like?

"My sister said he likes students who do their homework before class. I guess he doesn't like students putting their hands up for questions while he is talking, either. He gets very gruff when that happens."

"Knowing that is very helpful. What time of the day do you have his class?"

"I have him right after homeroom in the morning, which is not my best time. I have a hard time waking up."

"How about Ms. Schwester, your English teacher? What is she like and when do you have her class?"

"I have her right after lunch at 12:30 PM. I've heard that she is very nice, and that she likes students who ask questions. Her tests are hard, but you can take it again if you mess up the first time. I feel shy about asking questions, but I want to learn how to do that in her class. She's my homeroom teacher, too."

"What have you heard about Mr. Strommer?

"He's a new teacher. I have him for two classes, math, and science. These subjects are my best subjects, so I'm not too worried about them. I want to be more courageous about raising my hand when he throws out a question, though."

"We've gathered some useful information here," I pointed out. "Your goals are embedded in your concerns about your seventh grade year and the descriptions of your teachers. We will visualize mastering the fears you have about Mr. Hiccomb. This includes finding a way for him to see you as a good student. He is probably an "upfront" teacher. He likes homework done at the beginning, and he wants his students to be listeners. So, if you have questions, touch base with him at the beginning of class. You'll have to find a way to wake up in the morning so you are sharp and attentive in his class. We'll visualize you being that kind of student.

"Ms. Schwester appreciates the reputation of being liked. Showing appreciation will go a long way in building a good teacher-student relationship. She likes responsive students, so we'll visualize you raising your hand to answer questions.

"Finally, you have Mr. Strommer your math and science teacher and basketball coach. Generally, teachers like students who enjoy their subject and that's to your advantage. You have a good aptitude for math and science. Also, teachers who coach like students who are leaders, especially those who give 'assists' to other players and students. All you have to do is be yourself, do your assignments, and be helpful to others.

"The first step before we do the visualization is becoming relaxed, and I'll talk you through Progressive Muscle Relaxation (PMR). [3] The visualization will follow the relaxation. Once we have visualized or rehearsed success, we'll tell each body part to wake-up. I will give you

---

[3]

a handout with the visualization statements and Progressive Muscle Relaxation so you can practice at home. Do this at least once a day, preferably twice a day. Let's begin the PMR.

Progressive Muscle Relaxation

Find a comfortable spot and begin talking to your body. Tell it to settle into deep relaxation. When you talk to your body, say the following:

"I'm going to start with my toes and go all the way to the top of my head and tell each body part to feel *CALM, PEACEFUL, QUIET, and RELAXED.*

I will start with the toes on my right foot, the instep, the sole of my foot and my heel. I will tell them to feel *CALM, PEACEFUL, QUIET,* and *RELAXED.* From the knee to the thigh, I will tell to feel *CALM, PEACEFUL, QUIET,* and *RELAXED.*

The toes on my left foot I will tell to feel CALM, PEACEFUL, QUIET, and RELAXED. My ankles to my knees, I will tell

to feel CALM, PEACEFUL, QUIET, and RELAXED. The whole torso area with all of the internal organs, I will tell to feel *CALM, PEACEFUL, QUIET,* and *RELAXED.* The heart, the lungs, the esophagus, the stomach, the intestines, the kidneys, and the bladder, I will tell to feel *CALM, PEACEFUL, QUIET,* and *RELAXED.*

The right hand, the thumb, the fingers, the palm of the hand and the wrist I will tell to feel *CALM, PEACEFUL, QUIET,* and *RELAXED.* From the wrist to the elbow, I will tell to feel *CALM, PEACEFUL, QUIET,* and *RELAXED.*

From the elbow to the shoulder, I will tell to feel *CALM, PEACEFUL, QUIET,* and *RELAXED.*

The left hand, the thumb, and fingers, the palm of the hand and the wrist, I will tell to feel *CALM, PEACEFUL, QUIET,* and *RELAXED.* From the wrist to the elbow, I will tell to feel *CALM, PEACEFUL, QUIET,* and *RELAXED.* From the elbow to the shoulder, I will tell to feel *CALM, PEACEFUL, QUIET,* and *RELAXED.*

The right shoulder and the left shoulder, I will tell to feel *CALM, PEACEFUL, QUIET,* and *RELAXED.*

The chin, the mouth, the nose and the eyes, I will tell to feel *CALM, PEACEFUL, QUIET,* and *RELAXED.* The forehead and the top of the head and the back of the head, I will tell to feel *CALM, PEACEFUL, QUIET,* and *RELAXED.*

Now, my whole body from my toes to the top of my head has been told to feel *CALM, PEACEFUL, QUIET,* and *RELAXED.*

At the end, take three *DEEP BREATHS* saying as you inhale, "I am" and as you exhale say, "relaxed."

Let's visualize Joe starting school, the first day of his seventh grade year. He has practiced visualizing himself as a good student who is likeable and gets good grades. He has overcome his fears of Mr. Hiccomb. He knows that he is a teacher who likes attentive listeners and students who get their homework done and handed in at the beginning of class. He also knows that if he has a question about his homework or something in the previous lecture, he will ask the questions before class. Joe now sees himself as an attentive, wide awake student who listens to Mr. Hiccomb.

In Ms. Schwester's class, Joe feels relaxed because he has learned to appreciate Ms. Schwester's efforts to be likeable. He knows that this is a good place to practice being appropriately assertive, to ask questions and to give answers. It takes courage to raise his hand and answer, but he has visualized himself as a confident student and he is learning to overcome his shyness.

Next, Joe sees Mr. Strommer and he to be a good match. Joe enjoys both math and science class and his teacher senses his enjoyment. Mr. Strommer and Joe understand and respect each other. He excels in his classes and this success carries over onto the basketball court.

Joe sees himself as a successful student at the end of the year and as someone who has athletic skills. Because he became an active and an attentive student, he sees himself as a successful student. He is valued by teachers and students alike because he is helpful. When Joe looks back on his seventh grade year, he sees it as the best school yet. He enjoys the feeling of confidence and success.

Now, it is time for Joe quietly to move from the state of relaxation to the wake up state. He will start with the toes on the right foot and the left food and tell those parts to *wake up*. Just as before, with the relaxation exercises, he will visualize and work with each area of his body. From the ankles to the knees we'll tell to *WAKE UP*. From the knees to the thighs we'll tell to *WAKE UP*. The whole torso area, the heart, the lungs, the stomach we'll tell to *WAKE UP*. The shoulders and the neck area we'll tell to *WAKE UP*. The chin, the mouth, the nose, and the eyes we'll tell to *WAKE UP*. The forehead and the top of the head and the back of the head we'll tell to *WAKE UP*. Now our whole body from the toes to the top of the head has been told to feel *CALM, PEACEFUL, QUIET,* and *RELAXED*. We visualized a successful seventh grade year because Joe learned to be a competent, and attentive student. Throughout the year, we visualized him gaining respect from his teachers and fellow students. We visualized happy successful times during this school year. Then, we transitioned from the state of relaxation to the awake state. We told each body part to *WAKE UP*. Now, I would like you to take three deep breaths. *BREATHE: INHALE - HOLD - EXHALE (3 times) END OF VISUALIZATION.*

Taking a deep breath, holding it and exhaling slowly three time ends the visualization session. The success of this method is extraordinary, and was used most often in the fall for school anxiety and phobias. Feedback was overwhelmingly positive for the students.

Parents as Visualizers

Very young children are terrified by many experiences; the big school building, the first encounters at family gatherings, and Halloween costume parades. One of the most helpful visualizations parents can do is what I call "priming the pump." This helps to foster and enlist the child's successful participation in school activities. Most of all, it reduces the anxiety precipitated by these new encounters. There are two steps to this visualization:

Step 1 – parents need to communicate the big picture, or the overall expectations of the event. For example, you might explain a school open house to meet the teachers like this: "Johnny, you and I will go into the big front doors of the school. We can hold hands if you want. We'll walk down the hall together until we get to your classroom. You can show me where your desk or table is. When your teacher isn't talking to anyone, I would like you to introduce us. You say, 'Mrs. Wilson, I would like you to meet my mom and dad.' We'll shake hands with her and we'll talk a bit. Then, you can show us some of the papers and the artwork you have done. When it's time to go to the gym for punch and cookies, we'll walk down to the gym together. If you want punch and cookies, stay with us. If you would prefer to play with a friend, this is a time to do it. After a while, it will be time to go home and we'll go out the same door we entered."

Once this is shared, it is not so overwhelming for the child, but remember, this is just the overview. By explaining the process to your child, he will feel even more at ease knowing you are in charge.

Step 2 – When the time comes for the open house, break down each segment into "chewable chunks" and give positive verbal reinforcements. For example:"Johnny, the first step is going through the big doors to the school." Johnny and his parents proceed through the doors, "Good going, Johnny. Now, the next step is walking down the hall together to get to your classroom." Johnny takes his mother's hand and they walk down the hallway together. "Great, you remembered that you could hold my hand if you wanted." As they enter his classroom, Johnny's mother says: "Where is your desk?" Johnny shows his mother and father his desk. "Your desk looks nice and clean and you can see the board very well from here," his father says. "Now, Johnny, we would like to meet your teacher. This is what you say as we walk up to her; "Mrs. Wilson, I would like you to meet my mom and dad." Johnny freezes as his mom and dad approach the teacher. "That's okay, " his mom says, "just say 'Mrs. Wilson," and Dad and I will do the rest." Johnny takes heart and says, "Mrs. Wilson, I would like you to meet my mom and dad." He remembers and his mother proudly says, "Good job!"

As they leave his classroom, she reminds him to go to the gym for punch and cookies. Johnny takes his mother's hand gleefully. Once in the gym, his mother gives him a choice. "Do you want to stay with us and have cookies and punch, or do you want to play with your friends? After thinking for a minute, he says, "I want to go over and play with David." Johnny does just that and says goodbye to David when his mother comes to take him home. It's a very successful evening for Johnny and his parents.

This "two step visualization" can be used for most social occasions; a Christmas program in church or school, a family reunion, or a shopping trip. The child gains confidence because the parents explain what will happen at the event. The best outcome from this visualization training is the trust developed between the parents and the child.

Visualization is a useful tool as we face life's challenges, so *visualize, visualize, visualize*!

Kathryn Den Houter Ph.D.

Study Questions
Visualization

These questions have been carefully crafted to help you get to your transilient self. Answer them the best you can if you are working alone. If you have the support of a group, so much the better, since these questions are designed for group discussion. The topics you choose to visualize are as unique as each individual. Here is a lengthy list to give you some ideas of what you might like to address.

- Relationships (with friends, with family, with children, with animals.)
- Beliefs and values that you want to pass onto the next generation.
- Attitudes toward your body, health and mental health.
- Attitudes toward your upbringing and your child self.
- Facing your fears and anxieties.
- Valuing yourself and nurturing the self-esteem of others.
- Being in touch with your feelings and expressing them assertively.
- Your financial health. Learning to live within your means.
- How you behave toward people you like.
- How you behave toward people you don't like.
- Choice of occupation.
- Quality of workmanship.
- Attitude toward wealth.
- Truth telling and a desire to be honest.
- Intellectual development and educational attainment.
- Spiritual Development
- Choice of lovers
- Choice of spouse.
- Fitness goals.
- Other_____

Activity 1: Circle three areas that you in which you would like to grow and gain confidence. Write up a visualization for each of them. First, start by doing PMR (Progressive Muscle Relaxation) and, then, read the visualization expressing how you see yourself growing positively in this area. Finally, tell each body part to *wake-up*.

Activity 2: Make your own list, unique to you. Address those issues that make you feel uncomfortable. Visualization can help alleviate the fears and anxieties.

Chapter Eleven
The Far-Reaching Significance of Self-Esteem

"Always remember that conflict is essential for a good movie script." Mae Meld said. She was a seasoned professor at a local university conducting a seminar on How to Write a Successful Screenplay. I scratched my head, squinted, and decided to raise my hand.

"I think choices come before conflict. To my way of thinking, this makes choices more important than conflict." The students turned around to look at me, Mae paused for a time, quietly thinking. "You've got something there," she said. "Choices do make the conflict, they embody it and, without the conflict generated by choices, there would be no story line. Choices are important. They determine whether you live your life with high self-esteem or if you live your life trolling at the bottom."

Conscious, well-thought-out choices create a life of positive self-esteem. Nathaniel Branden in his seminal book, *The Six Pillars of Self-esteem*[1] advances six key components of high self-esteem. I have included a seventh one based on my clinical observations. The following is a list of those seven.

---

[1]

1. Becoming <u>conscious</u> of the choices that we make

2. <u>Self-accepting</u> self-talk is essential for positive self-esteem

3. Taking <u>responsibility</u> for your behaviors and attitudes

4. Learning how to be <u>assertive</u> and stand-up for your values

5. <u>Goal setting</u> and becoming proactive rather than reactive

6. Being <u>comfortable in your skin,</u> because talk and behaviors match

7. Cultivating a <u>spiritual</u> life that fosters self-discipline.

The first ingredient of positive self-esteem is making conscious choices. Here is a real life story that illustrates the importance of good self-esteem.

Susan Smith, a young mother from Union, South Carolina was driving her burgundy Mazda with her two sons, Michael (3) and Alex (14 months) in the back seat.[2] Her thoughts became desperate and dark, thinking about what her new boyfriend had said about her sons standing in the way of their relationship.

Susan considered her children baggage. She had to take care of her sons 24/7, and she wasn't getting the help from her ex-husband. After all, she needed someone to take care of just her. Susan was terrified of being by herself with children needing her day and night. All alone and

[2]

despairing, she hatched a plan to get rid of her "refuse." She strapped her children in their seats, loosened the handbrake, and let her car roll into John D Long Lake.

Susan Smith was born Susan Leigh Vaughan on September 26, 1971. She was an attractive, bright young lady and a good student at the University of South Carolina. Her unconscious behavior and low self-esteem bedeviled her. She convinced herself that she had to do the unthinkable to survive. Her unconscious choices made her knee-jerk through life. She based her unconscious behavior on what she saw happening in her family.

Her parents Linda and Harry Vaughan, were divorced when she was six years old and, just five weeks later, her father committed suicide. Soon after the divorce, her mother married a wealthy businessman who, as Susan's stepfather, admittedly molested her throughout her teenage years. Unfortunately, it has been suggested that her mother was more concerned about public humiliation than the wellbeing of her daughter, so she didn't get help for her.

Susan attempted suicide, twice, during those tumultuous years. She became promiscuous, having sexual relationships with three men, one of them married. In her late teens, Susan dated her friend, David Smith, became pregnant and then married him just before the birth of her oldest son Michael in October, 1991.

Susan's behavior mimics her upbringing. Using people and discarding them when difficulties arose was a common practice in her home. Families with sexual abuse present objectify their members.

The country was horrified by this senseless crime, but actually, it is more common that we dare to imagine. People can make horrific unconscious choices based on how they were raised rather than making conscious choices that promote healthy self-esteem.

The first characteristic of low self-esteem is a common denominator for criminals in our communities. Fraiberg, Adelson and Shapiro, in their paper titled, *Ghosts in the Nursery,*[3] discuss this unconscious process. We replicate what our parents did to us as children. You've probably heard people say, "When I open my mouth, I hear my mother/father talking." It could be your parents or it may be any "voice" from the past that haunts you when you are raising your own children.

These are the inter-generational transmissions of past trauma and pain. Feeling and acknowledging this pain makes us sensitized to the hurt. By acknowledging this pain, we become conscious of it and we don't want to pass this on to our children. We want to stop the hurt dead in its tracks. High self-esteem parents make this conscious choice and instead, find ways to nurture positive self-esteem in their children.

The second aspect of positive self-esteem is choosing to not be at odds with ourself. Some of our fiercest battles are fought internally. Guilt, shame, self-blame, grudges, disappointments and rivalries constitute the quarrels of our inner demons. Silence promotes listening to what is going on inside. If these thoughts are toxic and self-defeating we swim in "mental bacteria." We clean this up by practicing self-forgiveness, and self-compassion. Internal talk influences how we judge ourselves. Are we harsh in our evaluation of ourselves or are we filled with loving kindness? Can you have too much self-esteem? Look at it

---

3

this way; can you have too much health? The answer of course is no, you cannot have too much self-esteem. Don't be fooled by the pretenders. The actions of someone with a narcissistic personality disorder makes them seem like they have too much self-esteem, but this cockiness belies deep insecurities. This is not the true self-esteem. This is false sense of self.

The third component of positive self-esteem is accepting responsibility for one's self. Being mindful that you are the only one that can make you happy or unhappy, is a necessary step toward high self-esteem. Blaming others for your unhappiness only exacerbates your dependence on them. Sometimes, we nurse our past wounds and perpetuate our own victimhood by choosing to stay stuck in the "you done me wrong" state of mind. As we press forward to create a life of high self-esteem, we realize the importance of being proactive rather than reactive. This is especially evident in the next two qualities of positive self-esteem which are assertiveness and living with a purpose. For example, if someone is so drunk that they have no control and careen carelessly off the road into three cyclists, is he responsible for the injuries and loss of life? Yes, of course he was, even though he was not aware of, or conscious about, what he was doing. He didn't purposely try to kill them, but because he didn't take responsibility for his actions, he is responsible for the loss of life. So much unintended damage happens when we fail to live responsibly.

The fourth quality of someone with positive self-esteem is being assertive and standing up for one's values. The key component here is self-respect. As in other areas of self-esteem, there is a consciousness that comes from taking the time to "listen" to the context of the concern.

For example, Mary, a student at a local high school had a "bone to pick" with her cheerleading coach. Mary was always put in the bottom row of a human pyramid, and the coach always chose "large Louise" to be on her back. Mary groaned and wouldn't show up for practice the next day out of protest. She stewed only to herself about the unfairness of it all. During a half time performance at a basketball game, Mary took her place on all fours, Louise ended up on her back as usual. Just as all three layers were stabilized, Mary's right elbow gave way and the pyramid crashed causing the top of the group to plummet headlong into the floor. Fortunately, no one was seriously hurt, but the coach was furious and talked to Mary about safety and the responsibility of being a team member. Mary's lack of self-respect undermined her relationships with her coach and teammates. Her low self-esteem and lack of assertiveness was the culprit. High self-esteem Mary would have been assertive early in the practice sessions. Her feelings of not being treated fairly would have been addressed because she was being treated unfairly. Here is an example of assertive dialogue. It starts with "I" and then you add how you feel and why you feel that way. "Coach? Do you have a minute?" Mary would ask. After an acknowledgement from her coach, assertive Mary would say, "I feel unfairly treated and my body is sore because Louise is so heavy that my back hurts when we finish the pyramid. The next day I can hardly move." This effective communication implies high self-esteem because Mary is owning her feelings and her expression is direct and clear. She shows self-respect because she cares for herself and others.

The fifth aspect of positive self-esteem is living a life that is goal-directed. It has a plan and a purpose. Once a direction is determined, setting goals is key for judging yourself fairly. The internal dialogue changes when you establish realistic goals. It is a type of mental measurement because, when you successfully accomplish a goal, there is a little voice inside of you that says, "I can do it." When repeated successes occur, other inner voices say, "I can rely on myself. I am trustworthy. I can set out to accomplish this goal and I did it, so now I can believe in myself. I am my own best friend. I like myself." This is the sum total of high self-esteem. We all know of someone who planned to write the next "Great American Novel" and it never happened because they got lost in life. They were forced to work at Burger King to keep body and soul together, or they had to go back to school to get a degree, or training, that could translate into a job. This is quite common, yet discouraging pattern to those with high aspirations.

We also know people who have consciously set realistic goals and have been successful in a writing career. This happens every day. Goals that are attainable are a powerful tool for clarity of focus which ultimately secures high self-esteem. Each time we accomplish a step in our goal statement we are triumphant because we become trustworthy with ourselves. Step-by-step and goal-by-goal we acquire a self-appraisal that reminds us we are reliable and trustworthy.

The sixth characteristic of a person with high self-esteem is authenticity, which is described as being "whole" and "undivided." In other words, you are the same person during the day that you are at night. There is integrity because you have accepted *all* of yourself. You are transparent.

Geoffrey Chaucer, an English writer from the fourteenth century, illustrates this process of integration in a lovely tale about Sir Gawain and Lady Ragnell.[4] Lady Ragnell, an exceedingly homely woman soon to be the bride of Sir Gawain, was placed under an evil spell by her treacherous and ignoble brother, Sir Gromer. Sir Gawain took her to be his wife to save King Arthur.

Later at night in their wedding chambers, the Lady Ragnell said, "Sir Gawain, now that we have wed, show me your courtesy with a kiss. If I were fair, you would not delay. I pray you do this at my request with all due speed."

"I will at once; that and more!" he replied as he sped around to kiss his bride, only he saw before him not the loathsome creature he had married, but the fairest creature he ever did see. "Aye!" he cried out. "What are ye? A witch?" "I am your wife." "Ah, lady, then I must not be in my right mind. Earlier today you were the foulest sight that ever I saw—pardon me for saying so—and now, it seems my good fortune to have you, thus!" He rushed into her arms, giving her many kisses. "Sir," she said, pulling away for a moment, "There is more you must know. Several years ago I was deformed by enchantment by my brother, the terrible Sir Gromer. My beauty, as you see it now, will not hold. You need to choose whether you will have me fair by night and foul by day or else have me fair by day and foul by night. With the enchantment, it cannot be both. What do you choose?" "Alas!" said Gawain, "the choice is hard. To have you fair by nights and no more, that would grieve my heart

_____

4

139

right sore and if I desire by days to have you fair, then nights I'm sure I could not bear. So, I must put the choice in your own hands. Whatever you choose, as your husband that choice will also be my own." "Mercy, courteous knight! Of all earthy knights blessed must you be, for now the evil enchantment is released completely! You shalt have me fair both day and by night, and ever as I live I will be fair and bright. For the only thing that could release me from Gromer's spell was if a husband granted me, of his own free will, sovereignty to choose what I wish for myself. And now, Sir Knight, courteous Gawain you have done just that. You have granted me sovereignty, that which every woman wants above all else. Kiss me, Sir Knight, now, and pray thee be glad! "And, so, the Lady Ragnell remained beautiful all day and all night, and she and Gawain the Knight lived happily thereafter. The End. When we become transparent with ourselves, our self-esteem rises because we are truthful, unencumbered by the fear of exposing our dark side because it is already visible. There is honesty in doing and saying what we ultimately do. The conscious choice to integrate offers us the freedom of living authentically.

Finally, the seventh quality of high self-esteem is the discipline that comes from cultivating a relationship with God. Daily devotions remind us that we are loved and free from our miserable sins. Christ's sacrifice has made us free. The guilt and shame that clings to us like sweaty underwear no longer has control over us because we are cleansed. This transcendental dimension promotes a resilient life of high self-esteem.

Finding that transilience minimizes the time we need to recover after defeat and hardships. We learn to avoid judging ourselves harshly by choosing loving-kindness. The time we spend with our Lord underscores our self-esteem because he loved us so much. This transcendental dimension promotes a truly resilient life. Daily devotions strengthen us as we meet the challenges we face. Because we have been forgiven, we can forgive others and can choose to nurture the self-esteem of others. These spiritual components dovetail into a deep-seated self-acceptance.

Study Questions
Far-Reaching Significance of Self-Esteem

These questions have been carefully crafted to help you get to your transilient self. Answer them the best you can if you are working alone. If you have the support of a group, so much the better, since these questions are designed for group discussion.

1. On a scale from 1-10—1 being "not at all" and 10 being very conscious–indicate what number would apply in the following categories.

Relationships		Choice of Lover	
Leisure		Choice of Career	
Finances		Spiritual Life	

2. What behaviors can you change to gain more self-acceptance?

3. Do you take responsibility for your happiness? If not, what can you do to change that?

4. Are you assertive in all areas of your life? Indicate two areas that would benefit from greater assertiveness.

5. Write a mission statement that reflects your purpose for living. Develop two starter goals that would move you closer to your mission.

6. Are you honest with yourself? If not, share two or three areas that need work.

7. Are you transilient? How can you foster self-esteem with your spiritual life?

Chapter Twelve
Reverse the Curse

*Seekers of truth find redemption when they change
the words of their life.*
Kathryn Den Houter

Our words shape us. Negative word-curses enter our lives from many sources. It can be from parents, teachers, pastors, "friends," or just our own inner talk. Because our brain is so complex, we don't have the power to understand our own brains. Consequently, we have to make these nuances conscious. In other words, we have to *think* about how we think. To rise above our circumstances we have to remove the word-curses that are chaining us to lower ground.

Some word-curses are obvious because we have been wrangling with them for a long time. Others are subtle and hard to bring to the light of consciousness. Ten stubborn, hard to manage curses can be identified by these self-statements:

1. I'm afraid I will be left all alone. (fear of abandonment)

2. I have a suspicious mind (trust issues)

3. I can't stand on my own two feet. (chronically dependent on others)

4. I will always be poor and picked-on (catastrophic thinking)

5. My feelings never matter. (emotionally deprived)

6. I don't fit anywhere. (excluded socially)

7. I am flawed and deficient. (loser perspective)

8. I need to obey or I will be picked-on. (enslaved by the abuses of others)

9. I work hard, but it's never enough. (unrealistic standards)

10. I'm angry because I never get what I want. (privileged expectations)

Jeffrey Young, Ph.D. and Janet Klosko, Ph.D. in their book, *Reinventing Your Life*,[1] detail effective ways that can change the words of our lives. Once these curses are conscious, good relationships soon follow, thoughts are free from fear, we extinguish self-defeat, and master our feelings of anxiety and depression. To determine which problem persists in your mindset, please put the appropriate number in the blank beside each question.

---

[1]

Reverse the Curse Questionnaire

1. No, that's not me at all!

2. Very little sounds like me.

3. Somewhat descriptive of me.

4. Very close to describing me.

5. Yes indeed, that's me!

Abandonment

1. I cling to people because I worry that I will be alone.

2. I am jealous when a loved one talks to others- I fear being left out.

Trust issues

3. I don't trust others.

4. I am suspicious fearing others will violate me.

Vulnerability/victimhood

5. I worry that I'll be sick or harmed.

6. I have poverty thinking-I worry I'll never have enough.

Dependency

7. I rely on the kindnesses of others - I don't see myself as self-reliant.

8. I come from "helicopter-parents" who are always hovering.

Emotionally deprived:

9. I have never felt the deep intimacy of someone close to me.

10. No one ever meets my emotional needs.

Not belonging

11. I'm an odd-duck. I don't fit in.

12. I'm awkward and dull.

Flawed/not valued

13. If I share who I am, no one will ever love me.

14. I feel inferior and unworthy of other's respect.

Kathryn Den Houter Ph.D.

Inferiority

15. I'm just not as bright as others.

16. My skill level is just not as in demand as others.

Dominated by others

17. I have to obey others, or they will get even with me.

18. I over-extend myself to others, but neglect myself.

Driven by unrealistic goals

19. I must excel and be superior.

20. I have to keep working because there is no time to relax.

Privileged exception mindset

21. Laws are not indelible. Some of us can see right through the law.

22. I can't discipline myself to complete anger-provoking boring tasks.

Taking the above quick survey can help determine the negative self-talk that perpetuates the self-curse. When we have a pattern of thinking that runs counter to positive mental health, we must find a way to avoid creating a mindset that is destructive. Having high scores in one or several of these areas suggests a need for a change in how we talk to ourself. For example, if thoughts rehash the abandonment cycle, the following might be the self-talk: "I avoid close relationships because they never work out and I feel more lonely when the relationship ends."

Rewording this statement would provide blessings instead of curses. Here's an example: "With each relationship, I learn something new about myself and the other person. With this new knowledge, my relationships improve."

Instead of being governed by a fear of abandonment, life becomes a journey of discovery. It instantly changes one's attitude, and makes one more approachable.

Another problem is high scores in the trust area This indicates a self-talk that centers on mistrust and this impacts how we respond to others: "I have to protect myself or avoid them because I am sure that he/she will try to take advantage of me." A healthier self-talk might be,

"I will be open to what they have to say, think about it and determine if it is helpful to me or not."

The following are examples of negative self-talk followed by a healthy rewording:

Dependency: "I just can't do it on my own, I need someone I can lean on."
Rewording: "I have been able to solve some problems successfully, and I can do my best to solve other problems by myself."

Kathryn Den Houter Ph.D.

Emotionally Deprived: "I am never loved just because of who I am."
Rewording: "When I am relaxed and comfortable in my own skin, other people feel comfortable around me."

Not fitting in: "I'm so odd and clumsy that I don't want to be around people."
Rewording: "I will find a group that has the same interests that I have."

Flawed and not valued: "I am never given credit because I don't measure up."
Rewording: "I am just as capable as others, and I will respect myself."

Inferior: "I just can't perform the way others can because I'm dumb."
Rewording: "I have learned many skills, and I will continue to gain wisdom."

Controlled by others: "By always obeying others I feel safer."
Rewording: "I value my critical thinking skills so I will evaluate each situation carefully so I am true to myself."

Driven by unrealistic standards: "To be successful, I must work hard and always stay on high alert."
Rewording: "I am already successful. I will learn to relax."

Privileged exception mindset: "I get angry when dealing with the ignorance of others."
Rewording: "Patience is a virtue and the time I take to understand people is valuable time."

How we talk to ourselves has *enormous* influence over how we interact with ourselves and others. The first step is to determine how we are sabotaging our strengths and then, transforming our curses into blessings. The sum total of this is changing the words of our lives.

Kathryn Den Houter Ph.D.

Study Questions
Reverse the Curse

These questions have been carefully crafted to help you get to your transilient self. Answer them the best you can if you are working alone. If you have the support of a group, so much the better, since these questions are designed for group discussion.

1. What thinking patterns have challenged your growth?

2. Write down some of the negative statements that you say to yourself. What triggers these statements?

3. Reword these thoughts to regain a conscious hold on your thinking process, so your words create self-blessings?

4. What are some creative activities you can do to halt the negative junk mail thinking?

5. Write down five self-blessing statements.

Chapter Thirteen
Grief Recovery

Never before had I experienced such success as a therapist as when I introduced identifying and treating the losses in the client's life. Often, the impact of loss is what brings people into therapy. Loss is the most common experience we have, but we know the least about how to recover from grief and loss. Studies on how to age well conclude that the most salient quality of longevity is one's ability to process and overcome loss.

Understanding and managing grief is part of that undertaking. Discussing and treating loss normalizes therapy because loss is so prevalent and common. Any shame people harbor about not coping with their life's problems disappear when they see grief and loss as an everyday problem and they redefine their difficulties.[1] The first step for the client is to become aware of his/her losses. This identification process involves self-examination, since many losses defy conscious thought. Once losses are identified, then I introduce the book by John James and Russell Friedman titled, *Grief Recovery Handbook*[2] as part of treatment.

Because loss is so universal, addressing it is paramount for successful treatment. If not addressed, therapy will not

---

[1]

[2]

be effective. For instance, the borderline personality can bewilder therapists. Noting how losses affect their life is essential. Part of their insecurities stem from an inability to process loss. They don't see the connection between the losses and their behaviors. Their perception of life is skewed because they have spent their time reacting to something that they don't understand and can't articulate.

Because there are so many faces of grief, it is hard to nail down a definition, but here are three that have been proposed by Russell Friedman:

1. "Grief is the normal and natural emotional reaction to loss or change of any kind. Of itself, grief is neither a pathological condition nor a personality disorder." This is the most common definition, but several aspects are left out. It doesn't address feelings, it doesn't address every day losses, nor does it address how loss affects psychological conditions. This next definition includes the emotions and thoughts.

2. "Grief is the conflicting feelings caused by the end of or change in a familiar pattern of behavior." When someone dies, we are left with a major change that disrupts our normal pattern of daily living. Our emotions conflict because two opposite feelings are side by side. For instance, when we care for an ailing loved one, we experience deep sadness when they are gone.

A feeling of relief can be linked with this grief because of the overwhelming responsibility of keeping them alive. When recovery is hopeless, the caretaker becomes exhausted and empty, so relief is a very understandable feeling.

Another very different example is when we marry. Marriage is such a joyous occasion, but there is loss. It is the loss of freedom and the single life. Along with marriage comes a huge change that can play havoc with our usual patterns of behavior. These are conflicting feelings because joy and loss reside side by side. It requires finding a new normal and processing the losses.

It takes a bit of scrutiny to identify losses because so many of them we tuck away out of sight, while we just walk right on by others. It is necessary to process grief otherwise it accumulates and then, when a major loss happens, it comes back to haunt us and accentuates the magnitude of the loss.

Here are some experiences that create intangible losses which precipitate grieving.

- a loss of childhood due to an early loss of innocence
- a loss of respect, a loss of a dream, loss in an athletic competition
- a loss of face
- a loss of a pet
- a loss of status
- a loss of security
- a loss of trust …

The list goes on and on. People grieve these losses whether it is done consciously or unconsciously. Many times, in relationships, there is a grieving and a re-grieving. For example:

3. "Grief is the feeling of reaching out for someone who's always been there, only to discover when I need her (or him)

one more time, they're no longer there." Our patterns of behavior are hard to change, so we keep reaching out hoping to connect with that person. There is another more troubling behavior and that is reaching out for someone who never has been there hoping that they might finally come through for the first time. This is grieving and then, a *re*-grieving. The cycle is repeated over and over again until, hopefully, awareness pushes it to the conscious level so they can recover from the grief. Almost as a corollary to number three above, re-grieving might be described thus:

3a. "Grief is the feeling of reaching out for someone who has never been there for me, only to discover when I need them one more time, they still aren't there for me." This isn't because someone has died, it is because it's a continual reminder that the relationship is dead or that there never was a relationship.

John James and Russell Friedman deal expertly with mourners showing them how to "complete" a loss so they can stop the cycle of pain. Once we learn how to overcome loss we discard a lot of anxiety and depression. The first step is navigating through the inane the comments people make after someone has died. This is part of becoming conscious of the grief.

"Don't feel bad, you just need to give it time," is one example. *What does that mean? Is it that I shouldn't grieve? Perhaps it means that I shouldn't have any emotions especially unhappy ones. What does "you just need to give it time," mean? Should I just travel through each day without feeling because it will magically go away?*

"Just keep busy and don't think about it" is another comment. *So would it help if I just stop thinking and feeling and delay the inevitable? Do I go into frantic activity and push out my emotions? How would that work for me?*

Comments that are just implied by a look, perhaps, have even more dire consequences. For instance, if an adult scowls at a youngster who cries because of a loss, the child is shamed into hiding his/her feelings. The harsh unspoken message is "Don't trouble me with your tears, grieve alone." One of the cruelest responses to grieving is the loss of childhood innocence due to sexual abuse. When tears or anger surface, the abuser wants to minimize his/her actions by disrespecting the victim which causes a re-victimization, hurting the victim all over again.

Once the person who is grieving becomes aware of the need for healthy grief recovery, the next step is the Loss History Graph. This is a "timeline of losses" which starts with the first memory and continues to the current year. Major losses are indicated on this time line as is the intensity of those losses. The losses that evoke the most pain are highlighted and considered incomplete.

The next step on the grief recovery journey is making the losses more complete. For instance, so many of my clients have said, "I wish I had told my wife/husband how much I loved them. I realized that so much more after I lost them." The methods that heal this ache are the relationship graph and a completion letter.

The relationship graph is a time line for losses with that particular loved one. It starts with the first meeting and continues until the time of the loss. The completion letter includes apologies for hurtful actions and missed opportunities, including statements of forgiveness for hurtful actions that your loved one directed toward you. This is a painful, but truly healing, process that changes the incomplete loss to a more complete one. By writing the letter, the pain of the loss is diminished.

How do you overcome loss? One of the first actions in the grief recovery journey is writing down your losses, starting from your first memory. Make a timeline or a list. When grief is not dealt with it accumulates and then, when a major loss happens, it sends a shudder through one's emotional life and accentuates the magnitude of the loss. Start at the top of your list and listen to yourself to see if you register any pain from that loss. If you do, there still "incompleteness." Determine what unfinished business you have with your lost loved one and write a letter describing what you would do or say that would be different. In this way, you conjure up every painful loss and process it, until the list is exhausted.

Once this recovery process has been followed with each loss, you will notice a lightness of being, a joy of living and of the ability to dream new dreams.

Study Questions
Grief Recovery

These questions have been carefully crafted to help you get to your transilient self. Answer them the best you can if you are working alone. If you have the support of a group, so much the better, since these questions are designed for group discussion.

1. Complete a timeline of your losses. Start with your first memory, including the highlights of your life up until the present time. Circle the ones that evoke pain, since they are the ones that are incomplete.

2. Choose two losses to start with and begin by finding why they are incomplete for you.

3. Make the losses more complete by writing a completion letter which includes an apology, forgiveness, and what you would do differently if you had the chance.

Chapter Fourteen
Thankfulness

Here is a mental exercise for you. Try to think anxious thoughts at the same time you think thankful thoughts. Can't do it? That's because it's neurologically impossible to think anxious and thankful thoughts at the same time. Could it be that being thankful is the anecdote for anxiety?[1] Oh how I wish it was that simple!

Anxious thoughts have been practiced for many years and have been handed down from generation to generation, like a crazy quilt. It takes a lot of time and practice to overcome anxiety, but the practice of thankfulness is a good start, because so much of mental health is changing the script of our lives. We have to begin somewhere. Being thankful for what you do have is much better than living in fear and anxiety. Being thankful starts the rewriting of your life's script.

Consistently studies have shown over and over again that simple gratitude exercises such as keeping a gratitude journal or writing a letter of thanks can help us feel better. It substantially reduces depression and has positive lingering affects long after the exercise is completed. A brain-scanning study helps explain why this is. Prathik Kini[2], in

---

[1]

[2]

his study at Indiana University, recruited forty-three clients. Twenty-two of them had gratitude interventions. These tasks were varied, but all were characterized by thankfulness, generosity and gratitude. What the brain scans showed was increased sensitivity in the pregenual anterior cingulate area, which is known to be involved in predicting one's actions toward other people. Furthermore, it was found that these gratitude tasks were self-perpetuating in nature. The more thankfulness was practiced the more psychological benefits over the long term.

The findings were similar to a study that was done by Fox, Kaplan and Damasio in 2015.[3] They found that there were neural correlates of gratitude. In this experiement the subjects underwent functional magnetic resonance imaging (FMRI). The stories used to stimulate gratitude were from the Holocaust. The participants were asked to imagine themselves as Holocaust victims who received gifts of lifesaving food and clothing. These feelings of gratitude were then measured by the FMRI. The results revealed that rating of gratitude correlated with brain activity in the anterior cingulate cortex and medial prefrontal cortex. This study has given us a peek into the brain circuitry for moral cognition and positive emotion that accompanies the experience of benefitting from the goodwill of others.

Sarah Young[4] a writer of stimulating devotions expresses a keen understanding of thankfulness:

"Thankfulness takes the sting out of adversity. That is why I (God speaking through Ephesians and Psalms) have instructed you to *give thanks for everything.* There is an

---

3

4

element of mystery in this transaction: You give Me thanks (regardless of your feelings), and I give you Joy (regardless of your circumstances). This is a spiritual act of obedience— at times, blind obedience. To people who don't know Me intimately, it can seem irrational and even impossible to thank Me for heartrending hardships. Nonetheless, those who obey Me in this way are invariably blessed, even though difficulties may remain.

Thankfulness opens your heart to My presence and your mind to My thoughts. You may still be in the same place, with the same set of circumstances, but it is as if a light has been switched on, enabling you to see from My perspective. It is this light of my presence that removes the sting from adversity." (Ephesians 5 and Psalms 118 and 89)

Thankfulness counteracts anxiety, gives us peace, and helps us glide through adversity. By living with a thankful heart, we rise above our circumstances. A thankful mindset does not deny reality with its hordes of problems, but liberates the spirit by transcending above it. It gives us the gift of the big picture, discerning what is and what is *not* important.

The seven resilient qualities of connecting with nature, openness to change, dealing with the dark, overcoming scarcity with creativity, connecting with people, the power of reflection and finding a purpose are underscored by a deep spirituality. The lessons learned from the fifteen transilient personalities presented here is that thankfulness and transcendence became foremost in their journey toward transilience.

Study Questions
Thankfulness

These questions have been carefully crafted to help you get to your transilient self. Answer them the best you can if you are working alone. If you have the support of a group, so much the better, since these questions are designed for group discussion.

1. Take the challenge: try thinking anxious thoughts at the same time you are thinking thankful thoughts. What did you find out?

2. List five people for whom you are thankful. Is there a common trait among them?

3. Create a "Gratitude" journal. At the end of the day, list everything that makes you feel grateful.

4. How can you nurture thankfulness in others?

Appendix

Anxiety Inventory

1-Not at all, 2-Somewhat, 3-Moderately, 4-Often, 5-Very Often (Circle a number)

Weak or tired	1	2	3	4	5
Hot Flashes or Chills	1	2	3	4	5
Suffer Headaches or Neck Pain	1	2	3	4	5
Feel like you're Smothering	1	2	3	4	5
Feel lightheaded or off balance	1	2	3	4	5
Legs feel Rubbery	1	2	3	4	5
Shake or Tremble	1	2	3	4	5
Feel like there's a frog in throat	1	2	3	4	5
Sweat even when not hot	1	2	3	4	5
Muscles Tighten	1	2	3	4	5
Feel Agitated or Restless	1	2	3	4	5
Suffer from Constipation/Diarrhea	1	2	3	4	5
Frequent Stomach Upsets	1	2	3	4	5
Toes/Fingers become Numb or Tingle	1	2	3	4	5
Feel Tightness in your Chest	1	2	3	4	5
Heart Races or Skip Beats	1	2	3	4	5
Worry Something Terrible will Happen	1	2	3	4	5
Fear Disapproval	1	2	3	4	5
Fear Abandonment	1	2	3	4	5
Worry about Illnesses and Dying	1	2	3	4	5
Worry about Fainting or Passing Out	1	2	3	4	5
Worry you will Lose your Mind	1	2	3	4	5
Have frightening Fantasies	1	2	3	4	5
Have Racing Thoughts	1	2	3	4	5
Hard to Concentrate	1	2	3	4	5
Feeling Tense or Edgy	1	2	3	4	5
Have a Sense of Impending Doom	1	2	3	4	5

Kathryn Den Houter Ph.D.

Have Unexpected Panic Spells	1	2	3	4	5
Feel Detached from your Body	1	2	3	4	5
Feel like you're in a fog	1	2	3	4	5

This is adapted from Zung WWK, a Rating Scale for Anxiety, 1971.

TOTAL SCORE_____
DATE_____

Answer Key for Level of Anxiety

Total Score | Level of Anxiety

0-22 | None or very little anxiety
23-47 | Minimal anxiety
48-72 | Mild anxiety
73-105 | Moderate anxiety
106-130 | Severe anxiety
131-150 | Extreme anxiety/ panic

Depression Inventory

This is a brief screening tool for depression. If there is an indication of depression, contact your doctor.

1-Not at all, 2-Somewhat, 3-Moderately, 4-Often, 5-Very Often (Circle a number)

Unhappy or Dejected	1	2	3	4	5
Dread the Future or feel Discouraged	1	2	3	4	5
Feel Like you are a Loser and unworthy	1	2	3	4	5
Feel you are Inferior to Others	1	2	3	4	5
Judge Yourself Harshly and feel Guilty	1	2	3	4	5
Indecisive and Uncertain	1	2	3	4	5
Angry, Frustrated or Resentful	1	2	3	4	5
Lost Enjoyment in Life	1	2	3	4	5
Sluggish and Defeated by Life	1	2	3	4	5
Feel Unattractive most of the Time	1	2	3	4	5
Lost Appetite or Overeat	1	2	3	4	5
Insomnia or Sleep too Much	1	2	3	4	5
Lost Sexual Interest	1	2	3	4	5
Over-worry about Health	1	2	3	4	5
Wish you were dead	1	2	3	4	5

This is an adaptation of Zung Self-Rating Depression Scale. 1965.

TOTAL SCORE_____

DATE_____

Answer Key for Level of Depression

Total Score	Level of Depression
0-10	Minimal or very little depression
11-25	Functioning but feeling down
26-45	Mild depression
46-60	Moderate depression
61-75	Severe depression

Progressive Muscle Relaxation

From my experience, the best relaxation method is: find a comfortable spot, "talk" to your body, and tell it to settle into deep relaxation. When you talk to your body, say the following: "I'm going to start with my toes and go all the way to the top of my head and tell each body part to feel *calm, peaceful, quiet,* and *relaxed.*

You will start with the toes on your right foot, the instep, the sole of your foot and the heel. You'll tell them to feel *calm, peaceful, quiet* and *relaxed.* From the knee to the thigh, you'll tell them the same. Continue to the toes on your left foot, your ankles to your knees and repeat the process.

As you continue, you'll tell the whole torso area, with all of the internal organs—the heart, the lungs, the esophagus, the stomach, the intestines, the kidneys and the bladder—the same message.

Carefully repeat the process with the right hand, the thumb, the fingers, the palm of the hand and the wrist, to the elbow up to the shoulder.

As with the right side, you'll do the same with the left hand, the thumb and fingers, the palm of the hand and the wrist to the elbow, from the elbow to the shoulder.

Not forgetting the head, you'll move to the chin, the mouth, the nose and the eyes, the forehead and the top of the head to the back of the head, you'll deliver the same message of *calm, peaceful, quiet,* and *relaxed.*

Now, you have told your entire body, from your toes to the top of your head, this relaxing message. At the end, take three deep breaths, saying as you inhale, "I am" and, as you exhale, say, "relaxed." In this state of relaxation say, "I am confident, courageous and have healthy self-control."

Name_____ Date_____

Thought Distortion	Current Self-Statements	Healthy Rephrase

Name_____ Date_____

Thought Distortion	Current Self-Statements	Healthy Rephrase

Name_____ Date_____

Thought Distortion	Current Self-Statements	Healthy Rephrase

Endnotes

Preface

1. Austin Institute for the Study of Family and Culture, *Are Religious People Happier?* 2014

2. Koenig, Harold G. MD, Director of Duke's Center for Spirituality, Theology, and Health. Interview: Newsmax Health, (March 31, 2015.

3. Rohr, Richard. *Falling Upward* (San Francisco: Jossey-Bass, 2013).

Introduction

1. Goldman, Linda, *Raising Our Children to Be Resilient,* (New York: Brunner-Routledge, 2011)

2. Sandburg, Carl, *Carl Sandburg: His Life and Works,* (North Callahan: The Penn State University Press, 1987).

3. Kirkegaard, Soren, *Fear and Trembling Repetition,* (Princeton: Princeton University Press: 1983).

4. Bible: 1 Corinthians 9:25.

5. Frankl, Viktor, *Man searches for Meaning,* (Boston: Beacon Press: 2006).

Chapter One

1. Carson, Rachel, *Silent Spring,* (New York: Houghton Mifflin Company, 1990).

2. Louv, Richard, *Last Child in the Woods: Saving Our Children from Nature Deficit Disorder,* (Chapel Hill: Algonquin Books, 2008).

Chapter Two

1. Ulrich, Laurel Thatcher, *Well-Behaved Women Seldom Make History,* (New York: Vantage Books, 2008).

2. Standing, E.M., *Maria Montessori: Her Life and Works,* (New York: Penguin Group, 1957, 1998).

Chapter Three

1. Bible: Genesis 2:7, Job 33:4

2. Taylor, Barbara, *Learning to Walk in the Dark,* (New York: Harper Collins Publishers, 2014).

3. Ribowsky, Mark, *Signed, Sealed, and Delivered: The Soulful Journey of Stevie Wonder,* (Hoboken, NJ: John Wiley and Sons, Inc, 2010).

Chapter Four

1. Herndon, William Henry and Jesse W. Weik, *Abraham Lincoln: The True Story of a Great Life,* (New York: D. Appleton and Company, 1895).

2. Whitney, Henry Clay, *Life on the Circuit with Lincoln,* (Boston: Estes and Lauriat Publishers, 1892).

3. Griessman, Gene, *Words Lincoln Lived By,* (New York: Simon & Schuster, 1997).

4. Ibid.

5. Ibid.

6. Ibid.

7. Hallowverse online.

8. Ibid.

Chapter Five

1. Siiteri, Pk, Wilson, Jd, *Testosterone Formation and Metabolism during Male Differentiation in the Human Embryo.* Journal of Clinical Endocrinology and Metabolism 38 (1); 11305 (Jan 1974).

2. Tobin, James, *The Man He Became; How FDR Defied Polio to Win the Presidency,* (New York: Simon and Schuster, 2013)

3. Ibid.

4. Ibid.

Chapter Six

1. Morgan, Robert, *Then Sings My Soul: 150 of the World's Greatest Hymn Stories,* (Nashville: Thomas Nelson, Inc., 2003).

2. Dallimore, Arnold, *A Heart Set Free: The Life of Charles Wesley,* (Darlington, UK: Evangelical Press, 1988)

3. The Wesley Center Online: *The Journal of Charles Wesley,* (1736).

4. Ibid.

Chapter Seven

1. Frankl, Viktor, *Man Searches for Meaning,* (Boston: Beacon Press, 2006).

2. Cannon, Mae Elise, *Just Spirituality: How Faith Practices Fuel Social Action,* (Downers Grove, IL: InterVarsity Press, 2013).

3. Scott, David, *The Love that Made Mother Teresa,* (Manchester, NH: Sophia Institute Press, 2016).

4. Van Biema, David, *Mother Teresa's Crisis of Faith,* TIME, (August 23, 2007)

Chapter Eight

1. Beck Judith, *Cognitive Therapy, Corsini Encyclopedia of Psychology*, (published online: January, 30, 2010).

2. Ibid.

Chapter Nine

1. Holmes, Thomas and Richard H. Rahe, Journal of Psychosomatic Research. Vol. 11, Issue 2, August, 1967.

2. Woolfolk, Robert L. and Frank C. Richardson, *Stress, Sanity and Survival,* (New York: The New American Library, Inc., 1978).

3. Chopra, Deepak, *Ageless Realities, a Guidebook,* (Wheeling, IL: Nightingale-Conant, 1993)

4. Walter, Grey W., *The Living Brain,* (New York: Norton and Company, Inc., 1968).

Chapter Ten

1. Malta, Maxwell, *Psycho-Cybernetics,* (New York: Simon & Schuster, 1997).

2. Griessman, Gene, *Words Lincoln Lived By,* (New York: Simon & Schuster, 1997).

3. Jacobson, Edmund, *Progressive Relaxation,* (Chicago: University of Chicago Press, 1938).

Chapter Eleven

1. Branden, Nathaniel, *The Six Pillars of Self Esteem,* (New York: Bantam Books, 1994).

2. Wikipedia: Susan Leigh Vaughan Smith, 1971.

3. Freiberg, Selma, Edna Adelson and Vivan Shapira, *Ghosts in the Nursery,* (Child and Adolescent Psychiatry, Vol. 14, 1975).

4. Chaucer, Geoffrey, Canterbury Tales, (1387 – 1400).

Chapter Twelve

1. Young, Jeffrey Ph.D. and Janet Klosko, Ph.D., *Reinventing Your Life,* (New York: Plume, 1994)

Chapter Thirteen

1. Pitt, Brice, *Loss in Late Life,* PMC – U.S.National Library of Medicine – National Institutes of Health, BMJ, 1998, May 9; 316 (7142), 1452 – 1454.

2. James, John and Russell Friedman, *Grief Recovery Handbook,* (New York: Harper Collins Publishing Co., 2009).

Chapter Fourteen

1. Jarrett, Christian, *How Expressing Gratitude Might Change Your Brain,* (Online, Science of Us – blog, 2015).

2. Kini, Prathik, Joel Wong, Sydney McInnis, Nicole Gabana, Joshua W. Brown, *The Effects of Gratitude Expression on Neural Activity,* Indiana University, Bloomington, December 2015.

3. Fox, Glenn R., Jonas Kaplan, Hanna Damasio and Antonio Damasio, *Neural Correlates of Gratitude,* Department of Psychology, Brain and Creativity Institute, University of Southern California, Los Angeles: Frontier Psychology, September 30, 2015.

4. Young, Sarah, *Jesus Calling,* (Nashville: Thomas Nelson, 2004).

Kathryn Den Houter Ph.D.

Recommended Reading

Amen, Daniel G. *Change Your Brain Change Your Life.* New York: Harmony Books, 2015.

Barkley, Russell A. Defiant Children: A Clinician's Manual for Assessment and Parent Training, New York: Guilford Press, 2013.

Brooks, Robert and Sam Goldstein. *The Power of Resilience: Achieving Balance, Confidence, and Personal Strength in Your Life.* New York: McGraw Hill Books, 2005.

Branden, Nathaniel. *The Six Pillars of Self-Esteem.* (New York: Bantam Books, 1994.

Burns, David. *Feeling Good, The New Mood Therapy.* New York: Harper Collins, 1980.

James, John and Russell Friedman. *Grief Recovery Handbook.* New York: Harper-Collins Publishers, 2009.

Malta, Maxwell. *Psycho-Cybernetics.* New York: A Perigee Book, 2015.

Montessori, Maria. *The Absorbent Mind.* New York: Henry Holt and Company, 1995.

Montessori, Maria. *The Discovery of the Child.* New York: Ballatine Books, 1967.

Montessori, Maria. *The Secret of Childhood.* New York: Random House, 1966.

Standing, E.M. *Her Life and Works.* New York: Penguin Group, 1957,   1998.

Notes

Kathryn Den Houter Ph.D.

CPSIA information can be obtained
at www.ICGtesting.com
Printed in the USA
FSOW01n0216230417
33379FS